BIG PAPI

THE LEGEND AND LEGACY OF DAVID ORTIZ

CONTENTS

David Ortiz's two-run homer on April 12, 2016, produces a standing ovation.

The Boston Globe

Copyright © 2016 by The Boston Globe

No part of this publication may be reproduced, stored in a retrieval system, or transmitted in any form by any means, electronic, mechanical, photocopying, or otherwise, without prior written permission of the publisher, Triumph Books LLC, 814 North Franklin Street; Chicago, Illinois 60610.

This book is available in quantity at special discounts for your group or organization. For further information, contact:

Triumph Books LLC
814 North Franklin Street
Chicago, Illinois 60610
www.triumphbooks.com
@TriumphBooks

TRIUMPHBOOKS.COM
@TriumphBooks

Printed in U.S.A.
ISBN: 978-1-62937-347-8
This is an unofficial publication. This book is in no way affiliated with, licensed by, or endorsed by the MLB, David Ortiz, or the Boston Red Sox.

▶ **BOOK STAFF**
EDITOR Janice Page
ASSISTANT EDITOR Ron Driscoll

WRITER John Powers
ART DIRECTOR/DESIGNER Ryan Huddle

RESEARCHERS/PROOFREADERS
Paul Colton, Richard Kassirer, Ted Kehoe, James Matte, Joe Moore, James Page

FOREWORD

BY PEDRO MARTINEZ

I call David my compadre, my godbrother.

We shared the same agent [Fernando Cuza] when he was coming up in the minor-league system. We both grew up southwest of Santo Domingo, and I was always looking out for him because he was younger.

David is a unique kind of person and player, and he's never changed. One day, I dropped by a restaurant in Santo Domingo and I saw him receiving a phone call. I thought I was going to get the same David I was accustomed to seeing, with a huge smile, but instead he was a little bit sad and disturbed.

I asked him, "Why are you so down?" When he told me the Minnesota Twins had released him, I said, "Great." He said, "My daughter was born two weeks ago and I just got released. How can that be great?"

It was one of the few times I ever saw David serious toward me. I told him it was great because now I can get you to the Red Sox. From that moment, I kept trying to reach Theo Epstein, until I finally got ahold of him at 2:30 in the morning. I couldn't be prouder of having the opportunity to influence the Red Sox to bring him in.

David's attitude, the way he's performed in the big games, anything I can say will fall short. What David has done is unbelievable. Since he got to Boston, David was destined to have those opportunities, to carry the entire team to a championship.

It's the same with his attitude in the clubhouse. He learned a lot from me: Always treat everybody with class and respect. I went out there really determined to win and to try to do things right. David learned from that, he learned a lot from Manny Ramirez about hitting, and he's very grateful to have learned so much from all of us.

Even though we didn't pull it off in 2003, everything was in place for us to come back in 2004. The entire team had a never-give-up attitude and a lot of it had to do with David – he was always positive, always fighting.

I look at 2013, and people say that team overachieved. I don't see it that way – I would say they did what they set out to achieve. Boston is electric; it's a place that can influence anybody coming in to play. The beards that those guys grew reflected the harmony they had in the clubhouse. The bombing in Boston unified the entire nation along with David and the players to go out and achieve that 2013 World Series. Everything was destined to happen and David was at the center of it.

They say it's hard to play in Boston, but it all comes with the attitude. David and I are very similar – we're very outgoing, we're very happy campers, but we compete with the best of them and we are very serious about it when it matters. The things David was able to do identified him with Boston. It's a very good marriage between David and the fan base and the passion they have about their team.

I am extremely fortunate to have shared with David what looks to me like our destiny. We were destined to be together, to be in the right place at the right time, to share the same success. David and I were very fortunate to have come out of probably the roughest area that you can think of when it comes to poverty – both of us went through it, and I consider both of us blessed because we came out successful.

I can't wait to be sitting behind David five years from now, giving that [Hall of Fame] speech. David can also be very emotional – I can't wait to see how much joy he is going to show. To see him on the same team with me and the greats of the game, a team that no one will be able to separate us from – that's one I am looking forward to.

I will be a proud older brother.

Ortiz gives Pedro Martinez a hand as Martinez leaves a game in June 2003, and the pair embrace after completing their stunning 2004 ALCS comeback at Yankee Stadium.

Ortiz urges Red Sox fans to stay "Boston Strong" after the 2013 ALCS, and accepts his 2004 World Series ring from principal owner John Henry on Opening Day 2005.

INTRODUCTION

BY JOHN HENRY

When we took over stewardship of the Boston Red Sox in early 2002, many of the building blocks for success were in place: the game's most beloved ballpark, the most knowledgeable and by far the most passionate fans in baseball, a strong group of talented players, and a stirring rivalry with our closest geographical opponent.

But there were significant challenges. Our rival, the New York Yankees, had gone to the World Series four consecutive years, winning three times. The Sox hadn't won a World Series since 1918, and in 2001, won just 11 of their last 34 games.

Even so, we set out on what felt like a quixotic, epic quest to take on the Yankees and bring the World Series back to Boston – not once but repeatedly. That was our promise.

The Sox hadn't been on a level playing field with the Yanks since the 1940s. Change was needed, and right away. We pledged to revitalize Fenway Park and implemented a fresh organizational philosophy, one that involved making new, vital commitments to the community.

We won 93 games in our first season but failed to make the playoffs. We needed a difference-maker. We found a most improbable one in David Ortiz, who at the time was a 27-year-old slugger of modest credentials whose former team had dropped him, making him a free agent.

How David ended up signing with the Sox that winter before the 2003 season is remembered differently by those involved, which tends to happen when legends are recounted. What we do know for sure is that it was our ace, Pedro Martinez, who brought David to our attention, for which Red Sox fans will be forever grateful.

We now had a giant in our midst, one who lifted the Sox and an entire region onto his broad shoulders. David not only became one of the greatest clutch hitters in baseball history, he elevated the sport by the sheer force of his infectious personality. Who will ever forget the bear hugs, the omnipresent bling, the deep-throated laugh, the huge grin freely offered to teammates, fans – even opponents! That personality dominated every stage on which he appeared, whether it was on the field, in the community, on behalf of the David Ortiz Children's Fund or the Red Sox Foundation.

David not only played a transcendent role in the greatest comeback in sports history against the Yankees in 2004, with two walkoff hits in the span of one calendar day, but was the connective thread to the three World Series titles the Red Sox won in 2004, 2007, and 2013. His performance in the '13 Series, at age 37, ranks among the greatest ever, as he batted a majestic .688 (11 hits in 18 at-bats), reached base 19 times in six games, and was named World Series MVP. The Sox struck out 59 times in that series; David struck out once.

I remember a conversation we had at a party a couple months later, while sitting next to a Christmas tree.

"I don't understand why they kept throwing me fastballs," he said.

I answered, "Because no one could hit them. They were devastatingly good. But you did."

As none of us will ever forget, 2013 was a year of tragedy in Boston, its world-famous marathon senselessly attacked by terrorists, a tableau that sadly has been repeated in all too many cities around the globe. Our region and our baseball team coalesced into "Boston Strong" that year, David taking the microphone at Fenway Park and defiantly urging us all to resolve that we would not be cowed by terrorism.

Our entire season was infused with a purpose that went far beyond the winning of baseball games, which gave added poignancy to our celebration in October, the first time in 95 years that Fenway Park witnessed a Series clinching.

For me, for all of us, David's career has been nothing short of magical. There are so many stories like this one from his final season, when he promised a home run to an indomitable little boy named Maverick Schutte. Maverick was 6, David was 40, but they became fast friends after Kevin Millar, a mutual pal, introduced them. It was Millar who told David of how Maverick had undergone 30 surgeries after being born with a heart defect.

"Always stay positive," David told Maverick in a video that was sent to the child. "Keep the faith."

David pointed emphatically into the camera. "You take care, buddy," he said, "and I'm going to hit a homer for you tonight. Remember that. For you."

We know better than to expect our heroes to perform great feats on demand. But that night, David delivered, hitting the first pitch he saw in the eighth inning off Yankees reliever Dellin Betances for a tie-breaking, game-winning home run. Back home in Wyoming, Maverick watched and cheered.

"What I was trying to do," David told reporters afterward, "was make Maverick feel happy, and have that connection with him. You throw that out there, just to make sure he has a friend he can count on right here."

In 20 years in big-league baseball, the last 14 with the Red Sox, David made profound connections with all of us, connections that were personal, heartfelt, and meaningful. So fitting, truly, that we called him "Big Papi." Who knew that a baseball player could ever feel so much like family.

EARLY YEARS

DOMINICAN DRIVE AND A
MINNESOTA MISSTEP

BY JOHN POWERS

He originally wanted to be Michael Jordan.

David Ortiz was an imposing manchild who could make plenty of space for himself beneath a basketball rim. But if you lived in the Dominican Republic, your role models were Juan Marichal and Felipe Alou and the rest of the island's storied ballplayers. Once Ortiz vaulted the fence that separated the court from the diamond and swatted a home run in his first at-bat, he was hooked on horsehide.

Enrique Ortiz had been a promising pitcher but his burly son grew up swinging at bottle caps, doll heads, stuffed socks – anything that could pass for a baseball. By 16, David had been discovered by a local scout and passed on to the Florida Marlins, then an expansion franchise that was building a system from scratch.

"Dah-veed, you are going to play in the big leagues someday," his father assured him when he was cut loose, sore-elbowed, from the club's local prospects program after a few months. "Maybe it won't be with the Marlins, but that is their mistake. There are other teams to play for."

Ortiz ended up signing for $7,500 with the Seattle Mariners, who seasoned him for a couple of summers in the Arizona sun, then sent him to their affiliate

Ortiz, then a Twin, avoids a swipe tag by Red Sox second baseman Jeff Frye in a July 2000 game. Previous page: Fans watch a game at the "Lindos Suenos" or Beautiful Dreams field in El Mamon, Dominican Republic, not far from David Ortiz's birthplace of Santo Domingo.

in Wisconsin, where he was the Midwest League's best defensive first baseman (not a misprint) and hit .322 as the Timber Rattlers reached the 1996 championship round.

That made Ortiz an attractive trading piece and when the Mariners needed a third baseman for the stretch run, he suddenly found himself a Twin as the player to be named later in the Dave Hollins deal. "This was one of the best young hitters I've ever been around," observed Wisconsin manager Mike Goff, who said he "lost it" when he was told that Ortiz had been swapped.

Ortiz responded with a breakout year, zooming from A-ball to the majors in five months, hitting .317 with 31 homers and 124 runs batted in along the way. "He just stormed through our minor-league system," observed general manager Terry Ryan.

Minnesota, a losing club that needed offensive punch, plugged in Ortiz as its everyday first baseman in 1998. He was hitting .306 when he fractured the hamate bone in his right wrist, the slugger's occupational hazard, had surgery, and missed two months.

That was the beginning of an up-and-down ride in the Twin Cities that lasted for five years and was marked by injuries, confusion, and frustration. The mutual disenchantment between Ortiz and the club began

"YOU ARE GOING TO PLAY IN THE BIG LEAGUES SOMEDAY. MAYBE IT WON'T BE WITH THE MARLINS, BUT THAT IS THEIR MISTAKE. THERE ARE OTHER TEAMS TO PLAY FOR."

— **ENRIQUE ORTIZ,** AFTER SON DAVID HAD BEEN CUT BY THE FLORIDA MARLINS' AMATEUR FARM TEAM IN 1992 AT AGE 17

in spring training in 1999 when the Twins sent their 23-year-old strongman, who was hitting .137 with a dozen strikeouts in 51 at-bats, down to the Salt Lake Buzz for development.

After crushing Triple A pitching, Ortiz was back by September and in 2000 he was their main but miscast designated hitter, a basher for a club that wanted him to be a singles hitter. "Whenever I took a big swing, they'd say to me, 'Hey, hey, what are you doing?'" he recalled. "So I said, 'You want me to hit like a little (girl), then I will.'"

Ortiz never was quite sure what the club wanted from him and it didn't help that he and manager Tom Kelher face tattooed on his right arm. "All she worried about was how I hit the ball."

Then, after having knee surgery in the spring to remove bone chips, Ortiz missed several weeks and went 43 games without a homer. His turnaround came after the All-Star break when he heated up with a 19-game hitting streak while the Twins ran away with the AL Central and made the playoffs for the first time in more than a decade, knocking off the Athletics in the divisional series.

"I felt like things were really starting to come together," Ortiz said in his 2007 autobiography "Big Papi: My Story of Big Dreams and Big Hits." "I had the best year of my career, a season I dedicated to my mother... I was starting to make good money playing in the big leagues and I was starting to build my confidence, and I was playing for a team that went to the American League Championship Series. I really thought that things were looking up."

But his days in Minnesota were finished. The club had a Gold Glove first baseman in Doug Mientkiewicz. Ortiz, who was making $950,000, was up for salary arbitration and the Twins, a small-market operation with a limited budget, didn't want to pay him what could have been twice as much. So they let him go in December in what Ryan later conceded was "a bad baseball decision."

"I thought I might get traded or something but I never thought about getting re-

leased," said Ortiz. "It just didn't seem like the kind of thing that could happen. I was coming off a pretty good year and I was young and I thought there would be some team out there that would want to trade for a big dude like me."

Ortiz was a man with a point to prove in search of a wall to clear. The opportunity came in the Fens, where the Sox were revamping and, among other things, looking to replace Brian Daubach, whom they'd set free. Ortiz was four years younger, had similar stats, could split time at both first base and DH, and would play for less than half as much money. He also came highly recommended. Pedro Martinez called the Boston front office from Santo Domingo as soon as he heard that Ortiz was on the market and urged that he be signed; fellow countryman Manny Ramirez concurred.

After Ortiz pummeled the ball in the Dominican winter league and showed defensive deftness, club scouts urged general manager Theo Epstein to acquire him. There was little risk or expense and significant upside. "You're looking at a player with the potential to be a middle-of-the-lineup bat in the big leagues," reckoned Epstein, who inked Ortiz to a one-year deal for $1.25 million.

Ortiz became much more: the greatest clutch hitter in Sox history, who helped put three rings on his teammates' fingers; the supersized face of the franchise; and a civic icon.

ly weren't on the same page. "I don't think he really liked me," Ortiz mused later. "I don't know why. That was his style, not just with me. He was hard on young players. He was the kind of manager who likes veteran players. He never liked me."

When Ortiz broke his right wrist sliding into home against the Royals (yet stayed in the game and hit a homer in his next at-bat) and missed nearly three months of the 2001 season, it was the beginning of his *annus horribilis*. His mother Angela was killed at 46 in an automobile accident on the first day of 2002. "She used to love just watching me hitting the ball," said Ortiz, who had

BY ANY OTHER NAME, ALWAYS ORTIZ

BY NICK CAFARDO

avid Ortiz, known in 1996 as David Arias, was the top defensive first baseman in the Midwest League for the Seattle Mariners' farm team. And when Minnesota Twins general manager Terry Ryan acquired Ortiz from the Mariners for veteran third baseman Dave Hollins later that year, he felt he had stolen a top hitting prospect.

Ortiz proceeded to skyrocket through the Twins' minor league system in 1997, hitting .317 with 31 homers and 124 RBIs.

Five years later, after the 2002 season, Ryan released Ortiz. Ryan has beaten himself up ever since.

"We just made a bad baseball decision," Ryan said.

"I can't say David ever did one thing wrong. He was one of our best hitting prospects. We put him on our 40-man roster when he was in A ball. He just stormed through our minor league system; played at three levels in one year."

And what was Seattle GM Woody Woodward thinking?

David Arias (Ortiz was then using his mother's surname) hit .322 with 18 homers and 93 RBIs for Wisconsin of the Midwest League, while also earning defensive honors at first base.

"We had our people scout the league that year and David really stood out," recalled Ryan. "When Seattle needed a third baseman because of an injury, they came to us and we settled on David as the player to be named later."

Woodward seemed desperate when his third baseman, Russ Davis, was slowed by an injury. Hollins was a veteran having a good season for the Twins, and Woodward earmarked him as Seattle's choice. Ortiz was sent to Minnesota.

In Woodward's defense, he had four players — Alex Rodriguez (123 RBIs), Ken Griffey Jr. (140 RBIs), Jay Buhner (138 RBIs), and Edgar Martinez (103 RBIs) — having huge years. He had a first baseman — Paul Sorrento — with 93 RBIs, and Martinez was the greatest DH of his era. The Mariners scored 993 runs that season.

Ryan didn't have that abundance of offensive firepower.

A young Justin Morneau was behind Ortiz, but he was being converted from catcher to first base. Doug Mientkiewicz was an outstanding defensive player at first base, but the DH spot was open.

"DHs are pretty valuable, especially the ones who have done the things he has done," said Ryan. "You want a complete guy, but that wasn't a problem with us. There was plenty of room for a DH."

"Minnesota did a nice job identifying David as the player they wanted," Woodward said. "We needed a third baseman and Hollins came over and did a nice job for us. We had a lot of good hitters on the major league side, so it was hard to project David down the road on our club, but when he got to Boston . . . he's had a great career."

Ortiz was 19 when he played for Mike Goff for Wisconsin in the Midwest League.

"He was tough, but I really liked him and he taught me a lot," Ortiz said. "He'd fine me all the time. Twenty-five or $50 for things. I didn't have any money. But at the end of the year, he gave it all back to me."

Goff wouldn't say what the fines were for.

"If I'd reveal that, David would probably shoot me," Goff said. "He was a wonderful kid. I loved him. He had a great year for me. At the start of the season, I didn't have a first baseman or a lefthanded hitter. People in the organization said he was having throwing problems. I just said the kid had a good year in rookie league and I need a lefthanded hitter and first baseman. They said, 'OK, but he'll be a 24th or 25th guy on the team.'"

Ortiz nearly won the Triple Crown.

Wisconsin got into the playoffs that year and lost in the league championship.

"It was right after the [final] game, and my phone rang. It was one of our farm people and I said, 'Please don't tell me David is the player to be named in the Hollins deal.'"

But that's what they told Goff.

"I lost it," Goff said. "This was one of the best young hitters I'd

ever been around. This kid was special. Imagine if we had David and Edgar Martinez on the same team?"

In fact, when he gave Ortiz his cash back, Ortiz said Goff told him, "You know why I was so hard on you? Because of all the players on this team, you're going to be the big leaguer."

"I'll never forget that," Ortiz said.

Ortiz said back then, the Seattle organization didn't pay much attention to players who weren't high draft picks. Latin players, he said, had a tougher time getting through the organization. Ortiz said it was a long haul for those players.

And when he was traded, "I was devastated," Ortiz said.

Ortiz loved Martinez, a player who spoke to Ortiz a lot in spring training, much like Ortiz does now to young Dominican players.

Conversely, Ortiz has no affection for then-Twins manager Tom Kelly, and Ortiz doesn't think there was any the other way, either. Ortiz loved John Russell and Al Newman, two managers who had him in the Twins' lower levels. And Ortiz never blamed Ryan for dumping him.

"Terry is a good man," Ortiz said. "Decisions are decisions. Just because you make a bad decision doesn't mean you're a bad person. I have a lot of respect for Terry. The decision he made wasn't all his."

On Kelly, Ortiz said, "I don't think he really liked me. I don't know why. He was hard on young players."

Ortiz said longtime Twins

manager Ron Gardenhire, who replaced Kelly in 2002, "was OK. I remember one time in 1998 after the season, I remember Gardy told me, 'See you next year if you're still here.'

"The following year they sent me down on the first cut. A lot of people do things they forget about, but we don't forget. If you don't want people saying things about you later, don't say it," Ortiz said.

Ortiz also remembers a bad moment in Seattle. He said he was going to receive a bat at the Kingdome for being the best hitter in the Mariners minor league system. Lou Piniella, the Mariners manager at the time, was supposed to present him with it.

"I was all excited ahead of time because I'm gonna shake the manager's hand. [Piniella] comes out on the field and basically threw the bat at me and walked away. That was very disappointing. I was like damn . . . OK. That's how it is? It was something I never forgot," Ortiz said.

In Minnesota, Ortiz was pla-

tooning at DH with Matt Le-Croy. Ortiz finally broke out in 2002 when he hit 20 homers and knocked in 75 runs in 412 at-bats. He was going to get about $1.5 million in arbitration that year and the Twins decided to let him go. He settled with the Red Sox after they picked him up for $1.25 million.

Ryan disputes money was the factor.

"I hit 20 and knocked in 75 runs in 400 at-bats. Imagine if you give me 500-550 at-bats what that might lead to? I knew I was good. I knew I was a stud as a hitter, but I just couldn't prove it until I got the chance to play every day in Boston. And I had to wait for that because we had Jeremy Giambi," Ortiz said.

Theo Epstein had to be talked into picking up Ortiz by Red Sox international scout Louis Eljaua. Epstein balked because he had Giambi, but he still signed Ortiz. It was one of the best moves Epstein ever made.

"It's never been easy but that's good," Ortiz said. "That forces you to give everything you have. It's different when you have to fight your way through it. You don't take things for granted."

And as for his name, Arias or Ortiz?

"I haven't changed my name," Ortiz said. "When I was in Seattle they used to call me my mother's last name and sent my visa in my mother's name. When I got to Minnesota I straightened all that out. They said if something happens in the future we should call you by your father's last name. People think I changed my name, but I always went by Ortiz."

GLORY DAYS

BIG PAPI // THE LEGEND AND LEGACY OF DAVID ORTIZ

Ortiz hits a home run off the Yankees' Roger Clemens in July 2003, his first season with the Red Sox. Previous page: As the confetti flies, Ortiz salutes fans in Copley Square after the 2013 title.

BIRTH OF A LEGEND

BY JOHN POWERS

The first one was an autumnal preview of all the rest since. The Red Sox were down two games to one to the Athletics in the 2003 American League Divisional Series and were facing extinction at home, trailing 4-3 with two out in the eighth. Then David Ortiz, who'd been 0-for-16 with six strikeouts to that point in the series, launched a drive off future teammate Keith Foulke that bounced off the Oakland bullpen for the game-winning double, setting up his team to win the series on the road the next day.

"This is how guys are made heroes," observed first baseman Kevin Millar.

Thus did Ortiz make himself into Senor Octubre, the savior of seasons. All three of Boston's championship campaigns – 2004, 2007, and 2013 – bore Big Papi's timely thumbprints. None were more notable than the first of them, which ended 86 years of frustration and was made possible by Ortiz's consecutive wee-hour walkoffs that brought the Sox back from the dead against the Yankees in the American League Championship Series.

They were down three games to none after a brutal 19-8 home loss that concluded in a near-empty ballpark. "I thought about all the people I saw at the field that night, destroyed," said Ortiz, whose 10th-inning, two-out walkoff homer had clinched a divisional sweep of the Angels a week earlier. "I thought about us being in Boston. I

thought about how I don't like to lose. I'm not a loser."

So he won the next two games with two swings of the bat that turned the series around and produced the unlikeliest pennant in history. His 12th-inning blast off Paul Quantrill that landed in the New York bullpen at 1:22 a.m. set the stage for his game-winning, 14th-inning single the following night. "It was unbelievable," said outfielder Gabe Kapler. "It was Jordanesque. It was remarkable, unparalleled, unrivaled."

After his confreres went on to close out the Yankees in the Bronx, Ortiz set the tone against the Cardinals in the World Series with a three-run shot in the first inning of the opener, the first home run by a Sox player in the Fall Classic at Fenway since Carlton Fisk's blast against the Reds in 1975. "Who's your Papi?" Sox fans asked the visitors.

Pitching to Papi when the leaves were falling was a risky notion. After Ortiz jacked a two-run homer into the right-field seats to bust apart the opener of the 2007 divisional series

against the Angels, manager Mike Scioscia walked him intentionally with two outs and the score tied in the ninth inning of Game 2, then watched Manny Ramirez hit a killer three-run homer. "It's hard to let David beat you," mused Boston manager Terry Francona.

When the Sox went on to a mile-high sweep of the Colorado Rockies that year, Ortiz delivered the first run-scoring punches in the final two games in Denver. And during the storied 2013 worst-to-first run, perhaps the most emotional of all of

"YOU COULD SEE THAT ORTIZ WAS A GOOD HITTER IN MINNESOTA. BUT HE HAD HOLES. NOW THERE ARE NO HOLES, AND HE IS A LOT STRONGER."

— JOE TORRE, YANKEES MANAGER, AFTER ORTIZ HAD PRODUCED WINNING HITS IN GAMES 4 AND 5 OF THE 2004 ALCS

Boston's championship seasons, he was simply thunderous. His two homers off ace David Price in the second game knocked Tampa Bay backwards in the divisional series.

And after the Sox were floundering against the Tigers in the league championship series, on the verge of losing the first two games at home, Ortiz turned things around with one swing in the eighth inning, a game-tying, two-out, line-drive grand slam into the Detroit bullpen that upended outfielder Torii Hunter, his legs facing skyward, matching a Boston cop's arms-up victory salute a few feet away. "Storybook. Like a movie," said third baseman Will Middlebrooks after the Sox had gone on to even the series, which they won in six games. "Down and away and he hits it 400 feet. That's just stupid, right? It does not make sense. But that's David for you."

The man whose defiant declaration in the wake of the Boston Marathon bombing had helped rally the city made sure that the year ended with a triumphant parade down the same street. The Cardinals could not get him off the Series stage as Ortiz batted .688, reached base 19 times in 24 plate appearances, and was named Most Valuable Player. "What planet is that guy from?" wondered teammate David Ross.

Planet Papi is most visible after the fall equinox. His postseason numbers are otherworldly with a .295 average, 17 homers, and 60 runs batted in across 17 series. "I'm not a beginning guy," he once declared. "I'm an end-of-the-season guy."

From far left: A 2004 title ring; Big Papi wore a big belt for the 2013 parade, surveyed Boylston Street after the 2004 title, and played the field as needed when the Sox were in Philadelphia and other NL parks.

2003: Clockwise from top left: Teammates and coaches celebrate Ortiz's walkoff homer against the Orioles; Pedro Martinez and Ortiz do some scoreboard-watching; forced out in Game 5 of the ALCS; Ortiz's bat fails him in a June game; Johnny Damon gives Ortiz a hand in an August victory.

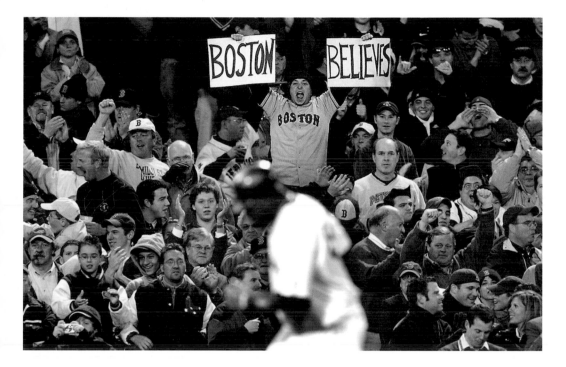

2004 POSTSEASON: A KEEPER

There's no way to fully explain or comprehend what came over David Ortiz in October of 2004. It was as if he'd struck some Faustian bargain with the baseball gods. Ortiz became the Walkoff Wonder, better than Babe Ruth, Mickey Mantle, Willie Mays, or Reggie Jackson.

In Greater Boston, we always thought of Carl Yastrzemski as the ultimate warrior of baseball's final month. Yaz didn't get many playoff opportunities, but he put up big numbers when it counted in 1967 and '75. He even homered off the unhittable Ron Guidry in the one game AL East playoff with the Yankees in 1978.

But the great Yaz never did what Ortiz did in 2004. No one ever did.

11
RBIs FOR ORTIZ IN 2004 ALCS

From Oct. 8-23, Ortiz enjoyed the greatest stretch of clutch hitting in postseason baseball history. He was Most Valuable Player of the AL Championship Series against the Yankees. He tied a record by knocking in 19 runs in the postseason – a record he reached in the first game of the World Series. He won three playoff games at Fenway with walkoff hits, within the span of 11 days. Two of his game-winners actually came on the same calendar day (Oct. 18).

Asked if he had a favorite moment, Big Papi smiled and said, "I only have one tape at home, the one the Red Sox made for us. I watch it over and over and over. When things are happening, you don't put attention to it, but when you're kicking back at home and you watch the DVD, you realize, 'Man, I can't believe I did that.'"

-DAN SHAUGHNESSY

2004:

Ortiz heads for first base after depositing his game-winning single in the 14th inning of Game 5 of the ALCS, and measures his game-winning home run off the Yankees' Paul Quantrill in the 12th inning of Game 4.

GAME 5, 2004 ALCS: THE MAN OF THE HOUR

Heroes? Got an hour? There was David Ortiz. There was David Ortiz. And there was David Ortiz. The big guy started his team on the way back from a 4-2 eighth-inning deficit when he redirected a Tom Gordon pitch into the Volvo sign atop the Monster Seats. That's a prodigious poke for a lefthanded batter, by the way. As for his game-winning at-bat in the 14th inning, it was downright Boggsian, and it testifies to the type of hitter Ortiz has become. For Esteban Loaiza was pitching not just well, but downright brilliantly, and Ortiz fouled off five tough pitches before his winning base hit.

"Best stuff he's had since he's been with us," said Yankee manager Joe Torre, and that's no hyperbole. Loaiza made tough pitch after tough pitch, right down to the one Ortiz plopped in front of Bernie Williams to bring home Johnny Damon (who had drawn a one-out walk and moved to second on a Manny Ramirez walk) with the winning run.

Torre had remarked before the game that, "You could see that Ortiz was a good hitter in Minnesota. But he had holes. Now there are no holes, and he is a lot stronger."

Only a sophisticated hitter could have had that at-bat, and only a very strong one could have muscled that particular pitch over the infield (think vintage Jim Rice).

-BOB RYAN

2005:
Clockwise from top left: A flying leap after his homer beat the Angels in September; a three-run homer tops the Orioles in June; Ortiz salutes his mother after a homer in the ALDS vs. Chicago; Ortiz rubs heads with Mike Timlin after a September win; sharing a spring-training cart ride with wheelman Kevin Millar, Manny Ramirez, and Jay Payton; Wally gets a tweak on the nose after a June win.

ORTIZ LED THE AMERICAN LEAGUE IN EXTRA-BASE HITS FOUR TIMES: 2004 (91), 2005 (88), 2007 (88), AND 2016 (87). HE WAS SECOND IN 2006, WITH 85.

2006:

Clockwise from top left: Escorting Jordan Leandre, 5, to sing the national anthem in April; solo homer vs. the Rays in September; teammates prank Ortiz by initially ignoring him after his 52nd homer; a walkoff homer beats the Indians in July; a postgame steal of the base after a stolen base in July; pressing the flesh after an August homer.

2007:
Clockwise from near right: Signing autographs before the September regular-season finale; showing off the October hardware; dugout greetings after a solo homer in July; saluting Manny Ramirez after an ALCS homer; bat drop after an August grand slam against the Angels.

"PEOPLE ARE USED TO SEEING YOU COME THROUGH ON EVERY AT-BAT AND DOING SOME DAMAGE. IT CAN'T ALWAYS BE THAT WAY. THIS IS NOT A NINTENDO GAME. THOSE ARE REAL PITCHERS OUT THERE TRYING TO MAKE A LIVING."

– DAVID ORTIZ, DURING AN INJURY-PLAGUED 2007 SEASON

2007 WORLD SERIES: LEADER OF THE PACK

2007:
Curt Schilling, Kevin Youkilis, and other mates greet Ortiz after a September walkoff homer against the Rays.

It would be impossible to overstate how critical David Ortiz was to Boston's championship run in 2007. He had become one of the most feared hitters in the game, and his presence in the lineup was a major benefit to those around him, specifically cleanup hitter Manny Ramirez. In the clubhouse, Big Papi was a dynamic, soothing personality who proved to be a confidant and friend to all, particularly the Latin players.

The Red Sox players respect Ortiz for his skills, but also his willingness to speak from the heart on their behalf. There is no bull with Big Papi; the big man prefers to tell it straight.

On the eve of the American League Championship Series, Ortiz lamented the lack of power on the Red Sox, pining aloud for the kind of lumber featured in the New York Yankees' lineup. Never mind the Yankees were already home, eliminated by the Indians in the first round.

"It can't always be me and Manny," Ortiz said. "We need some help, bro. I thought we would have gotten some [last winter]."

General manager Theo Epstein said the Red Sox front office had grown accustomed to impassioned Ortiz critiques and learned to put them in proper perspective.

"Sometimes I wake up and wish he didn't say some of the things he says," Epstein conceded, "but it almost always comes from a place of spontaneity and emotion. It never comes from a bad place.

"David really cares about winning. I never want to limit his emotion in any way, because he speaks from his heart. His personality has been critical to the success of our team. He brings all corners of the clubhouse together."

-JACKIE MACMULLAN

2008:

Clockwise from near right: Ortiz performs his home-run ritual in March in Tokyo; a homer in a rehab start at Pawtucket, after a wrist injury in July; hugging Johnny Pesky after Pesky's No. 6 is retired in September; exchanging caps with members of the Hanshin Tigers at the Tokyo Dome.

10

TIMES AN AMERICAN
LEAGUE ALL-STAR

23

FEWEST HRs IN A SEASON
WITH RED SOX (2008, 2012)
(BOTH INJURY-PLAGUED YEARS)

"THE WAY THAT HE TALKS, THE WAY THAT HE WALKS INTO A ROOM, ALL EYES TURN TO HIM."

– JOHN FARRELL,
RED SOX MANAGER

2009:

Clockwise from near right: Greeting Dustin Pedroia at spring training; a first-base laugh with the Orioles' Ty Wiggington; preseason work in the cage; batting vs. Boston College in Fort Myers; signing for a couple of adoring fans.

"THERE'S NO REPLACING A GUY LIKE DAVID."

— DUSTIN PEDROIA

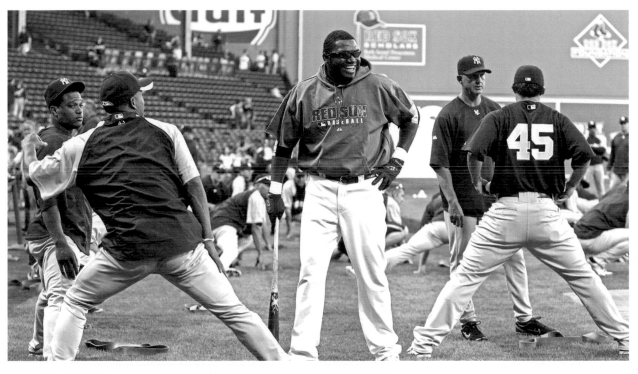

2010: Clockwise from far left: Doubling against the Yankees in May; roaming in enemy territory before the season opener with the Yankees; competing in the Home Run Derby In Anaheim before the All-Star Game (he won); tripling against the Jays in August.

2011:

A pat on the back for Dustin Pedroia in July; playing through the rain in May; circling the bases in Yankee Stadium after a homer off A.J. Burnett; view from the Green Monster seats for the home opener.

2012: Clockwise from far left: Snapping his bat after lining out against the Orioles in May; following through on a homer vs. Seattle; working out after an Achilles-tendon injury; walking with son D'Angelo at spring training; escorting Johnny Pesky and Bobby Doerr with Jason Varitek and Tim Wakefield on Fenway's 100th anniversary; seeking a fresh start in February with Kevin Youkilis and Adrian Gonzalez after an ugly end to 2011.

GAME 2, 2013 ALCS: AN EPIC GRAND SLAM

Close your eyes and it is 2004 all over again. Tom Brady is throwing last-second touchdown passes en route to a certain Super Bowl, David Ortiz is the greatest clutch hitter in baseball history, and the unwashed Red Sox are escaping from a hopeless deficit while Mayor Menino is pumping tires on the duck boats.

What might be the most exciting day in Boston sports history started with Brady's TD pass to beat the Saints with 5 seconds left and ended at festive Fenway at 11:44 p.m. when Jarrod Saltalamacchia singled to left, scoring Jonny Gomes from third to give the Red Sox an impossible 6-5, series-squaring, come-from-behind victory over the stunned Detroit Tigers.

In the day of all days, the moment of all moments was the Ruthian sight of Ortiz crushing a first-pitch, game-tying grand slam off Tigers closer Joaquin Benoit in the eighth inning. As right fielder Torii Hunter flipped spectacularly over the bullpen wall in fruitless pursuit of the flying seed, a Boston bullpen cop signaled "touchdown" and Fenway came to life.

This was not a walkoff. This was a liftoff. Flat on the ground for almost 17 strikeout-filled innings over two games, Boston's championship hopes were launched into the airspace over the Back Bay as 38,029 fans rattled Fenway's 101-year-old timbers.

"As we've seen, we're going to play to the final out," said Sox manager John Farrell. "David has come up big so many times in the postseason, none bigger than tonight.

Just an incredible comeback here."

"We needed it, man," said Ortiz. "I tried not to do too much. I wasn't trying to hit a grand slam. Just try to put a good swing on the ball. . . . I grew up playing with Torii. He's one of the best outfielders I've seen in my life. I think the ball took a left turn while he was turning right."

It was a Fisk-like moment.

Incredible? Unbelievable? Cosmic? Epic? Go ahead. Choose your word. This was right up there with any of the thrills we've seen at the ancient yard over the last century. Dave Roberts was summoned for the ceremonial first pitch and the event unfolded in a fashion reminiscent of the comeback against the Yankees in 2004.

In Foxborough or at Fenway, this was not a day to leave early.

All hope seemed lost at Yawkey Way. The Sox were striking out at a record pace – 17 times in a 1-0 defeat on Saturday and 13 more times in Game 2 as they fell behind, 5-1, through seven innings.

We were set to bury them. The Sox managed only one hit over the first 14 innings of the series. They were about to go down two games to none and face Justin Verlander in Game 3 in Detroit. After not losing four straight games all season, the Sox looked like candidates for a sweep in the ALCS.

It was 5-1 in the eighth when Tigers manager Jim Leyland got a little too cute and started a Joe Maddonesque parade of relievers. He wound up with big, nasty Benoit facing Ortiz with the bases loaded and two outs. Ortiz had already fanned twice on the night.

Papi struck on the first pitch. There was little doubt as his heat-seeking missile screeched toward the Sox bullpen. Hunter hit the wall at full speed and flipped as the ball soared beyond his reach. It was 5-5. It was already over.

"It's playoff baseball," said Leyland. "It looked like we had one in hand. We let one get away, no question about that, but these were two great games."

It cannot get better than this.

-DAN SHAUGHNESSY

2013:
The Tigers' Torii Hunter goes tumbling and Fenway erupts with Ortiz's grand slam in Game 2 of the ALCS; Ortiz homers off the Cardinals' Michael Wacha in Game 2 of the World Series.

2013: Clockwise from far left: Ortiz is greeted after sliding home on a Mike Napoli double in World Series Game 1; helping with the champagne toast after celebrating the world title on the field; fans exult after the Game 2 ALCS slam vs. Detroit; joining Mayor Menino after a ceremonial ALDS first pitch.

.688

BATTING AVERAGE (11 FOR 16) IN 2013 WORLD SERIES

GAME 4, 2013 WORLD SERIES: TALKING THE TALK

David Ortiz, chairman of the impromptu gathering, didn't clear it with his manager. In fact, he didn't even consider such a thing. Protocol? What do you mean, protocol?

After all, it was the middle of Game 4 of the World Series, and the chance of another Red Sox title was slipping away faster than any radar gun could clock it. All Ortiz knew was that it was his time to talk.

"David doesn't script much," said Sox manager John Farrell, who watched with a blend of delight and admiration as Ortiz rallied the troops at Busch Stadium in St. Louis. "And that certainly wasn't scripted."

After the Sox went on to win their third world title in 10 seasons, Ortiz's dugout speech, his Fall Classic carpe diem, pretty much stood as the Series' seminal moment.

Having fallen behind two games to one, the Sox were at the precipice of dropping two back in the best-of-seven series, their bats again turned meek by stout Cardinals pitching.

Enough of that, said Ortiz. The sole holdover from Boston's curse-busting team in 2004, he summoned his teammates, some of whom looked frustrated and forlorn, to one end of the dugout. It was time for them to wake up, shake the clouds of doubt, and sense the opportunity.

This was the World Series, the big man reminded them, and though not everyone wins when they get to October, there are scores of players, some among the game's greats, who never even get the chance to attempt victory.

"Like I told my teammates, 'If you think you are [always] going to come to the World Series, you're wrong, especially playing in the AL East,'" he said later, his poignant words having helped the Sox rally to a 4-2 win that would ultimately lead to two more victories and a six-game conquest of the Cards. "Do you know how many people we beat to get to this level? To this stage? A lot of good teams, a lot of good teams, man, and that doesn't happen every year.

"I told them, 'It took me [six] years to get back up to this stage, and we had better teams than what we have right now and we never made it. So take advantage of being here.'"

Such was the crux of the Ortiz message. Sense the moment, seize it, before the dream of slipping on a diamond ring turns into a lasting choker of regret.

"I just saw a lot of faces, you know, looking in the wrong direction," he said. "And every team has that guy [to speak up] and I think I am that guy here."

Thus, in that instant, he became not David Ortiz the designated hitter but Big Papi, prophet of horsehide-and-pine-tar resurrection. He talked. They listened. And they got it going, ignited by Ortiz's leadoff double in the fifth inning that was only the second hit off St. Louis starter Lance Lynn.

"His words were spot-on," said Farrell, who soon saw Ortiz wheel home with the run that tied the game, 1-1, on a Stephen Drew sacrifice fly. "I can't say everything that he said, but the message was spot-

.455

CAREER WORLD SERIES BATTING AVERAGE, BEST BY ANY PLAYER WITH AT LEAST 50 PLATE APPEARANCES

.576

CAREER WORLD SERIES ON-BASE PERCENTAGE, IN 59 PLATE APPEARANCES

2004, 2007, 2013
WORLD SERIES STATS

"THERE IS ALWAYS THIS CALMNESS ABOUT HIM. AND WHEN PITCHERS SEE THAT CALMNESS, I THINK IT WORRIES THEM."

— GABE KAPLER, SOX TEAMMATE FOR FOUR SEASONS

on. It was along the lines of, 'We've gotten to this point because of the players we are.' And I think what he was reflecting on is what we all sensed and felt, in that we weren't having normal or typical at-bats.

"It just felt like there was maybe an overarching mood that needed to be jolted and snapped out of, and that's what took place."

Ortiz ended the Series with a .688 batting average, but neither baseball-reference.com nor the Elias Sports Bureau keeps track of verbal grand slams such as the one Ortiz delivered in Game 4. In the inning after Ortiz's double helped bring the Sox even, Jonny Gomes submitted the kill shot, smacking a three-run homer over the wall in left for a 4-1 lead. The invisible tail on that comet had Ortiz's wisdom written all over it.

"Any time this guy steps in the box," said Gomes, "there's a presence. Any time this guy puts a uniform on, there's a presence. If this guy wants to rally us together for a pep talk, it was like 24 kindergartners looking up at their teacher. That message was pretty powerful."

All in all, said Gomes, the speech was the "little kick in the butt that we needed."

Infielder Xander Bogaerts just turned 21, the youngest of the Red Sox with a locker next to Big Papi. When Ortiz spoke, he was all ears.

"Whenever he talks, everyone listens. He's respectful to all of us and we give him the same respect. It was a pretty amazing moment."

It stands now as a moment that will last forever.

-KEVIN PAUL DUPONT

"WE PROBABLY DON'T HAVE THE TALENT THAT WE HAD IN '04 OR '07, BUT WE HAVE GUYS THAT ARE CAPABLE TO STAY FOCUSED AND DO THE LITTLE THINGS. AND WHEN YOU WIN WITH A BALLCLUB LIKE THAT, THAT'S SPECIAL."

– DAVID ORTIZ

2014:
Clockwise from near right, Obliging fans on arriving at spring training; stringing together title and MVP rings on Opening Day; gesturing toward the press box after a ball he hit was ruled an error in June; eyeing an opposite-field homer vs. the Angels; tagged out at home trying to score against the Cubs in July.

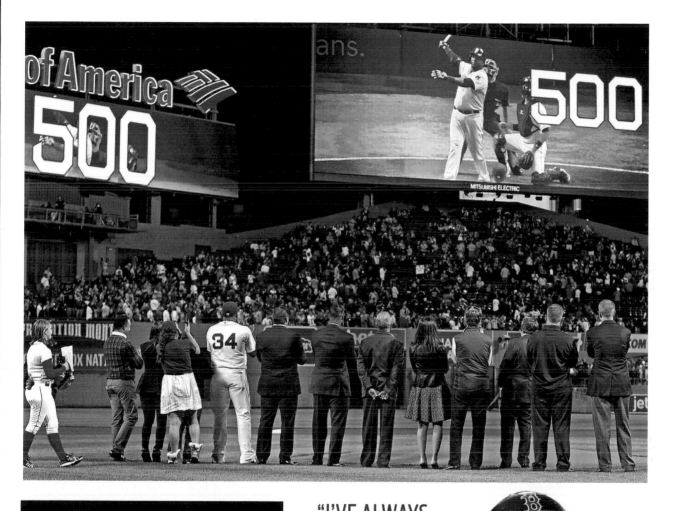

Belting an opposite-field homer vs. the Marlins in July; being feted for his 500th homer, which came nine days earlier, on Sept. 12 at Tampa Bay; fans celebrate No. 502 vs. the Rays on Sept. 24.

"I'VE ALWAYS BEEN MY OWN HITTING COACH."

– DAVID ORTIZ

Ortiz doubles and goes on to score the first Boston run in pivotal Game 4 of the 2013 World Series.

DAVID ORTIZ TOP 10 POSTSEASON MOMENTS

2003 ALDS, GAME 4 VS. ATHLETICS

EIGHTH INNING, LOSING 4-3, VS. KEITH FOULKE
Two-run double to right field scores Garciaparra and Ramirez, wiping out one-run deficit and sending the series to Game 5, which the Sox win, 4-3, to set up ALCS vs. Yankees. Ortiz went just 2 for 21 in the ALDS, adding a single in Game 5.

2003 ALCS, GAME 7 VS. YANKEES

EIGHTH INNING, LEADING 4-2, VS. DAVID WELLS
Ortiz's long solo home run provides Boston with a 5-2 lead, with six outs to go and Pedro Martinez on the mound. What could possibly go wrong? After the Yankees rallied to tie it, Ortiz added a double in the top of the 10th inning, before Aaron Boone's home run provided the crushing final blow in the 11th.

2004 ALDS, GAME 3 VS. ANGELS

10TH INNING, 6-6, VS. JARROD WASHBURN
Ortiz hits a walkoff home run to left-center field to complete the series sweep. "When I walked to the plate, I was thinking, 'Let me try to get this over with.' I reviewed all the at-bats I had against him and [figured] he might want to try to get me out with the cutting fastball. So I went looking for it, and he threw it to me, and I got it."

2004 ALCS, GAME 4 VS. YANKEES

12TH INNING, 4-4, VS. PAUL QUANTRILL
Walkoff, two-run home run into the Yankee bullpen ends a 5-hour, 2-minute game and gives Red Sox hope after they had lost the first three games of series, including a 19-8 debacle one night earlier. Ortiz's two-out, two-run single in the fifth inning off Orlando Hernandez had given the Red Sox a shortlived 3-2 lead.

2004 ALCS, GAME 5 VS. YANKEES

14TH INNING, 4-4, VS. ESTEBAN LOAIZA
On the 10th pitch of the at-bat, Ortiz fights off a ball in on his fists to drop a single into center field that scores Johnny Damon from second for Ortiz's second consecutive extra-inning walkoff hit. In the last of the eighth inning, Ortiz had homered off Tom Gordon to bring Boston within 4-3.

2004 ALCS, GAME 7 VS. YANKEES

FIRST INNING, 0-0, VS. KEVIN BROWN
With two outs and Ramirez on first after Damon had been thrown out at home plate, Ortiz blasts a two-run homer to give the Red Sox a critical early 2-0 lead on their way to a 10-3 victory and the first comeback from a 0-3 series deficit in baseball history.

2004 WORLD SERIES, GAME 1 VS. CARDINALS

FIRST INNING, 0-0, VS. WOODY WILLIAMS
Ortiz kicks off the World Series with a one-out, three-run home run to get the Red Sox on the board and off to an auspicious start. He added an RBI single in the bottom of the seventh to help the Sox establish a 9-7 lead, but the Red Sox squandered both leads before Mark Bellhorn homered for the victory.

2007 WORLD SERIES, GAME 3 VS. ROCKIES

THIRD INNING, 0-0, VS. JOSH FOGG
Ortiz doubles to score Jacoby Ellsbury with the game's first run, then comes around to score on Mike Lowell's single as the Red Sox continue their momentum from winning Games 1 and 2 in Boston. They win Game 3, 10-5, and complete the sweep the next night, as Ortiz again scores Ellsbury with the first run on an RBI single in the 4-3 win.

2013 ALCS, GAME 2 VS. TIGERS

EIGHTH INNING, LOSING 5-1, VS. JOAQUIN BENOIT
With the Sox having lost Game 1 and shown little offense in Game 2, the series – and the postseason – turned when Ortiz hit a line-drive grand slam into the bullpen on the first pitch he saw from Benoit to tie the score at 5-5. The Red Sox earned the walkoff win an inning later, then won three of the next four games to take the series, 4-2.

2013 WORLD SERIES, GAME 4 VS. CARDINALS

FIFTH INNING, LOSING 1-0, VS. LANCE LYNN
Trailing in the game and 2-1 in the Series, Ortiz doubles and scores the first Red Sox run of pivotal Game 4 on Stephen Drew's sacrifice fly after giving the team a scorching pep talk between innings. Ortiz went on to go 3 for 3 with a walk, and also scored ahead of Jonny Gomes on Gomes's deciding three-run homer. The Sox swept the final three games for their eighth world title.

-RON DRISCOLL

MR. PERSONALITY

BIG PAPI // THE LEGEND AND LEGACY OF DAVID ORTIZ

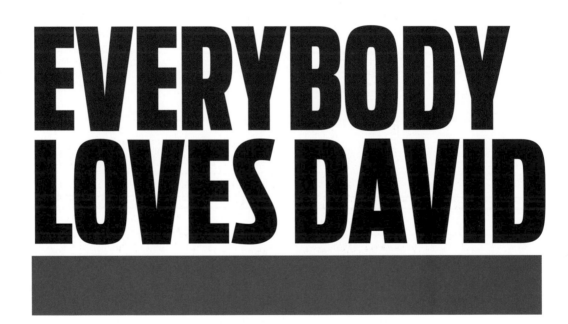

Ortiz holding a fan's baby during the national anthem before an August 2013 game at Kauffman Stadium in Kansas City; Previous page: Leading the way to the Marathon finish line at the 2013 rolling rally.

EVERYBODY LOVES DAVID

BY JOHN POWERS

The nickname came from his being the new guy in Fort Myers. "I couldn't remember anybody's name," David Ortiz recalled. "So I called everybody 'Papi' because that's what they do in the Dominican. It's just a friendly thing, a sign of respect. After a while they started calling me 'Papi' in return and then it became 'Big Papi.' It took off."

Only a few seasons after Ortiz arrived in Boston he no longer needed a last name. Big Papi was plenty. There was a Big Papi plane, a sandwich, and a hot sauce. Was there anyone who didn't know of him, he was asked after only two seasons here. "A child that was just born today?" he guessed puckishly.

Ortiz's size, smile, and style made him universally recognized and revered. "He's the most charismatic baseball player I've ever been around," said Yankee's designated hitter Alex Rodriguez, who called him "a big cartoon character." "Whites like him, blacks, Hispanics, everybody. Everybody loves David Ortiz."

Particularly those who knew him best – his teammates. "Personality-wise, the way he carries himself, the way he goes about his business, he's a true professional," pitcher Jon Lester once said. "From Day One that I've been here, he's never changed...You can't ask for anything more as a teammate than having David Ortiz in that locker room with you."

Papi's daily arrival in the clubhouse was an entrancing event. "The way that he talks, the way that he walks into a room, all eyes turn to him," said Red Sox manager John Farrell. "Not just because of his stature and what he's accomplished but the energy and life and fun-loving approach he has for the game and a certain situation."

Ortiz's tenure alone (14 seasons in the Fens) gave him patriarchal primacy. "Daddy's back," declared catcher Christian Vazquez when Ortiz turned up for his final spring training. When Boston won the World Series in 2013, Ortiz was the only man remaining from the fabled 2004 club and was treated as an oversize oracle. "If this guy wants to rally us together for a pep talk it was like 24 kindergartners looking up at their teacher," said outfielder Jonny Gomes.

He might not have been the captain, but Ortiz had a customized role. "I have three different jobs here," he said. "1. Designated hitter, 2. Cheerleader, and 3. Make sure that we have everything stay where we like it to be."

Because he appeared for only a handful of minutes in every game, Ortiz's mere emergence from the dugout was an occasion marked by possibility and puissance. "How many players in the game do you stop to watch him swing the bat?"

> ## "YOU CAN'T ASK FOR ANYTHING MORE AS A TEAMMATE THAN HAVING DAVID ORTIZ IN THAT LOCKER ROOM WITH YOU."
>
> — JON LESTER

mused Yankee second baseman Robinson Cano. "When you think of the Red Sox you think of him."

Ortiz was the gargantuan, gregarious, and grinning face of the franchise. "He brings a great spirit and sense of humor and a big, bear-like personality to the park," observed club president Larry Lucchino. "He leads the league in hugs."

Nobody made an entrance like Papi, garbed in skintight urban finery and Diesel shades and bedraped in diamonded bling from earrings to watches to wristbands to "DO 34" chains. "Best-dressed All-Star every year," said Orioles outfielder Adam Jones. "Not even close."

That style, which included muscle cars like the red Mercedes-Benz convertible that was his quarter-million-dollar present to himself after the 2004 title year, was what Ortiz called "how we roll."

So when his Minnesota teammates wanted to play a prank on him during an exhibition game, they filched his clothes, leaving him to cram-jam himself into a county worker's orange jumpsuit. "You should have seen him," said Doug Mientkiewicz, who later became Ortiz's teammate in Boston. "The suit was up to his shins. There were buttons popping off all over the place. He came over to our clubhouse yelling and hollering. That's an image I will never forget."

Big Papi always was a supersize special edition, the only one of his kind on the shelf. Bodacious, bedazzling, and beloved. "I've never heard one bad thing said about David Ortiz," said Sox second baseman Dustin Pedroia, "and I don't think I ever will."

A selfie on the South Lawn with the president in April 2014; a hug for Nomar after Garciaparra's three-run homer in September 2003; a dapper David receives the 2011 Roberto Clemente Award at the 2011 World Series.

In his hometown of Santo Domingo in January 2010, where a donation was made to the David Ortiz Children's Fund to support youngsters who need treatment from Heart Care Dominicana.

THE GUY BEHIND THE SMILE

BY AMALIE BENJAMIN

When David Ortiz enters a clubhouse, he strides in confidently, almost dancing. He looks as if he owns the world and, at this moment, perhaps he does.

He says this is who he is. He is the man with the smile, joking and yelling and grinning all at once. His personality reaches out, into the stands, through the TV, across a table. He says it in his clothing choices – the man prefers matching shirt-and-cap combos that are often about as loud as his voice.

"I think everybody pretty much knows what it's all about [with] me," Ortiz says. "I don't like and I don't believe in people who are pretty normal when everything is going well and they change when they see a bump in the road. I let them know straight up I don't like it. That's the way I am. I don't like lies. I don't like two faces. I don't feel comfortable with it. I'll tell you what

A celebratory splash courtesy of Hanley Ramirez after his extra-inning double beat the Astros in a May 2016 game; with Xander Bogaerts, helping to send Derek Jeter into retirement in 2014.

I feel in a heartbeat. That's me."

David Ortiz, on the field and off, does not hide.

That's part of the reason why the slugger was one of the most popular players in baseball, part of the reason why, only 2½ seasons after the Minnesota Twins decided he was not worth re-signing, Ortiz received more votes than any other player for the 2005 All-Star Game, picking up 4,138,141, including more online tallies than anyone else.

It's why he is beloved. Ortiz was never the enigma that Manny Ramirez was. He didn't have the stoic, no-nonsense persona of Jason Varitek. He wasn't confrontational and dramatic, except in his flair for producing the game-winning hit. Ortiz is what he is.

The only question is what made him that way.

Because Ortiz isn't smiling now. He isn't grinning, isn't shaking. He's sitting, simply, and pain washes through his eyes. He's talking about his mother and about how, since the accident, nothing can get him down. Because nothing, he says, will ever be quite so hard.

Angela Rosa Arias was killed in a car accident in January 2002. It was, absolutely, the most difficult moment in his life.

"At that point I have to be the stronger [person] in the family because, pretty much, my sister, my aunt, my uncles, my pop, pretty much everybody got hit really bad," Ortiz says. "I had to act like, 'Hey, let's hang in there.' I got to take the heat. I lose my mother, that I love, the person that give me the most love ever. But I never quit. I act strong in that one moment that was terrible. But I've got my pain. I deal with the situation. After that, I don't think I have faced anything worse than that, anything more painful than that.

"That's why I see everything in light and happiness."

This isn't the Ortiz of the ballpark. This isn't the Ortiz of the commercials, the ones that show him gregarious and laughing. This is the other David Ortiz. The one that he keeps inside.

"Life is a challenge," Ortiz said. "Life is a challenge that you need. There's things in life that are going to throw you into the ground, but if you learn how to get up, that means you are not a quitter. That's the best that a human being can have, never quit. If you quit, if you are a quitter, you're giving up on your kids, your wife, your family, you're giving up on them."

He says he's never done that, never given up, though he came close after his mother died. He won't, he says, if he hasn't yet.

He has taken that pain and transformed it into joy. It has been subsumed into the old Ortiz, the one before he lost his mother and lost his job in Minnesota almost at the same time. It was the one that started before and blossomed after, once the sorrow became less acute and life got, well, good. Even in a city as notoriously tough on its talent as Boston, Ortiz stayed Ortiz.

"I don't think the environment has anything to do with his personality," said Terry Ryan, Ortiz's general manager with the Twins. "If you go down to the Dominican, he's the same there. He's the same in Boston. He did the same in Appleton, Wis. He's always had a smile. He's got a flair about him. He's got a charismatic approach."

It isn't just his personality, of course. Ortiz has done more than enough at the plate to satisfy the legions of Red Sox fans who adore him, more than a few of whom walk around with his name branded across their backs. Ortiz has simply been transcendent in the playoffs through his career, often getting the hit at just the right time.

Ortiz effectively won the World Series for the Red Sox with his bat in 2004 and in 2013. And, just for that, he could be deified in Boston. In this town, his swings mean just as much as his smiles.

"If he stunk and he hit .150 and hit zero home runs and drove in nobody, people wouldn't have that," said Varitek in 2005. "The fact [is] that he's extremely good at what he does, one of the best in the game and he has that very likable persona. When you're mechanically sound, as he is, those slumps are short. That's what makes him so good."

He was good – and reliably consistent. Ortiz hit .287 or better eight times in his first 13 seasons in Boston, and he hit 30 or more home runs nine times in those 13 seasons.

"ORTIZ SWAGGERS INTO A CLUBHOUSE WITH A SMILE AND JOKE, A ONE-MAN MERENGUE FULL OF NOISY HAPPINESS AND DELIGHT, READY TO DRILL HIS NEXT VICTIM WITH A FOUR-LETTER LINE DRIVE TO THE FUNNY BONE."

– KEVIN PAUL DUPONT, BOSTON GLOBE SPORTSWRITER

A long time ago, when Ortiz was little, his father explained baseball to his son.

An escalator, he said. You rise with it, getting on when you reach the big leagues. Each step is an achievement: playing well, making the All-Star team, winning a World Series. He dreamed of winning a Most Valuable Player award as the final step in that progression, but the closest he came was in 2005, when he finished second. It appears that he will have to settle for "Most Popular."

"He went from being a good player to one of the elite hitters in the league," said Terry Francona, Ortiz's manager for eight seasons in Boston, from 2004 to 2011. "And then you add on his infectious personality, his ability to smile. He has the quickest, warm-est smile I've ever seen. He can make a person who walks through that door he's never met before feel so comfortable. And that is a gift. You couple that with his ability, you have David Ortiz."

Ortiz sits, thinking quietly in a clubhouse normally filled with thumping rhythms. His father slightly shorter, slightly rounder, is behind him, 20 yards away. Ortiz, still not smiling, considers his answer.

Is he ever not, well, him?

"Of course, as a human you get down," Ortiz said. "Everything is not only happiness. Everything is not flowers and a piece of cake. There's a lot of things in life that you see, that you have to face. That's life. But, otherwise, happiness."

And that, really, is David Ortiz.

THE MAN

BIG PAPI // THE LEGEND AND LEGACY OF DAVID ORTIZ //////

Pausing during batting practice in July 2016. Previous page: Sharing a 2014 spring-training moment with son D'Angelo.

THE PLAYFUL, PROUD FACE OF THE CITY

BY JOHN POWERS

It was a black-Hispanic immigrant from the Caribbean who helped bring together a shattered place five days after the 2013 Boston Marathon bombings. "This is our [expletive] city and nobody is going to dictate our freedom," David Ortiz proclaimed during a tribute to victims, survivors, and responders at Fenway Park before the Red Sox played their first home game after the tragedy. "Stay strong."

He was born in Santo Domingo and came to America to play a child's game. But it only took a couple of seasons for Ortiz to become a baseball hero and a few more years to be a civic icon. So his defiant declaration became Boston's full-throated

response to a terrorist act. "What we've been through this week, that was my feeling," Ortiz said. "I was hurting like everyone else. That's how I am."

When the Dominican Republic was inundated with water in the spring of 2004, Ortiz put a cardboard box on a table in the Sox clubhouse. "Please, any help you can donate to the people of my country — D.R.," he wrote. "They got hit by the flood."

His personal generosity to charitable causes in both of his homelands is boundless. The David Ortiz Children's Fund, established in 2005, provides critical pediatric care, including heart surgery, for young patients in both countries. "You get famous and you have what you need, but sometimes there's always something missing," he observed. "Right now I feel I'm a full package."

If the cause involved children, Ortiz always was quick to step up to the plate. "I love to be a kid," he declared after spending an afternoon playing Wiffle Ball and munching loaded sausages with 30 of them to fulfill a $30,000 auction donation to benefit Good Sports, a Dorchester nonprofit that gives sporting goods to city kids.

Papi's perennial playfulness in and out of uniform made him a cherished character hereabouts. When he became a U.S. citizen in 2008 it was a significant and symbolic story. "It's a great country," said Ortiz, whose wife and children were born in the States. "Proud to be here, now proud to be a part of it."

From the start, Ortiz and Boston embraced each other with open-armed affection. He was a symbol of the social transformation of the city, playing for the last ballclub to integrate in a tribal town that was being riven by racial unrest when he was born. Big Papi is a bilingual ambassador who's as comfortable in a Hyde Square barbershop as he is at City Hall, where he and the former Hizzonah were best buddies. "That's my man, you know," Ortiz said of the late Tom Menino. "Me and Menino, we go way back."

If Menino held the formal title, Ortiz was the unofficial mayor, eternally affable and approachable. In 2013, when he was named Most Valuable Player as the Sox won the World Series for third time in less than a decade, he finished third in the mayoral race with more than 500 write-in votes.

"I remember John Henry once told me that I was the only player he's ever known who really is able to play in Boston," Ortiz remarked. "And he's right. I know how to handle everything in Boston."

He was comfortable in a town that had great expectations of its ballplayers but faint memories of them delivering championships. That changed when Ortiz led the resurrection against the Yankees that led to the breakthrough 2004 title and established him as a civic colossus.

"This is as close a bond between a player and the city in the game of baseball," Sox president Dave Dombrowski mused early in 2016. "When you talk about what he accomplished, what the team accomplished, his ability and his length of time here, very few guys mean that much to this city."

Ortiz could have set down anywhere after the Twins cut him loose because his price was going up. He chose the city on a hill that had never seen anyone quite like him. "My life, I've been built up around this organization, this city, and these fans," Ortiz said. "The best thing that ever happened to me was to come play in Boston."

Joining Boston mayor Marty Walsh in helping five-term former mayor Tom Menino throw out the first pitch on Opening Day 2014; preparing for Game 1 of the 2013 World Series as a rainbow splits the sky.

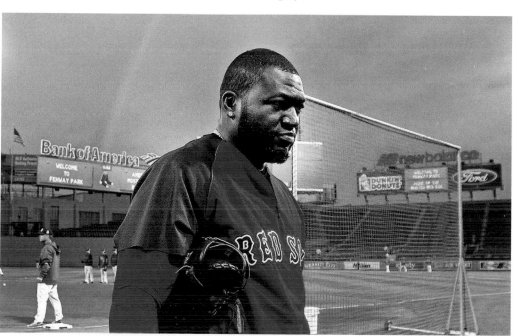

Ortiz greets Diana Reyes, 12, who was born with a hole in her heart, after Ortiz's fundraising efforts helped to provide for surgeries for her and other indigent children in the Dominican Republic.

A HEARTFELT GESTURE

BY STAN GROSSFELD

In January of 2006, David Ortiz was preparing for the baseball season in his hometown of Santo Domingo. Unlike previous seasons, there was a special urgency for the Red Sox slugger; as a member of the Dominican Republic national team, he knew his participation in the World Baseball Classic would cut into his spring training. There was no time for distractions.

But one day he took a break.

"My friend says, 'Hey, let's go to this one place, I just need five minutes from you,'" Ortiz recalled.

And that request helped save the life of 12-year-old Diana Reyes, who was born with a hole in her heart.

Dr. Fred Madera, a surgeon with the Heart Care Dominicana Foundation, which was established to aid indigent children with congenital heart disease, will never forget Big Papi's visit.

"He showed up [at the Hospital General de la Plaza de Salud in Santo Domingo]," Madera said. "He saw kids with purple lips and purple nails, because of a lack of oxygen. He started talking to the parents. 'Hey, you like baseball?' They said, 'Yeah, but my kid has never been able to play. He's gasping for air.'

"Then [Ortiz's] eyes got watery. This huge guy was very touched."

Ortiz saw a dozen kids that day. One wore a Red Sox cap and said his dream was to play baseball, but he couldn't.

"Ortiz noticed he was big," said Madera. "He said, 'That could be me.' He kind of wiped his tears — he cried. I thought, 'Hmmm. This big guy, I didn't know he had tears.' He said, 'Well, you're gonna play baseball,' and he signed a baseball."

Ortiz also saw a child who had just come out of surgery.

"He learned how one child's illness affected the whole family," said Nelvea Pelaez, executive director of Heart Care Dominicana. "The social impact is more than fixing a hole in the heart of one kid.

"We had to take him out. He had this look on this face — not looking at anybody, just gazing at the horizon. All he said was, 'I have to do something about this. I'll be back.'"

Less than a year later, Ortiz kept his promise and returned with a check for $200,000, enough to start the first pediatric cardiovascular unit in the Dominican Republic.

"When I saw David go into the intensive care unit, I didn't see a big star going in there," said Pelaez. "I saw someone letting their real feelings come through. When you see that, you say, 'Oh my God, this is an original — not like a politician or a movie star.'"

Ortiz isn't embarrassed to ac-

Ortiz visits with children and parents at the Hospital Generalde la Plaza de la Salud in his hometown of Santo Domingo after presenting a check for $200,000 to Heart Care Dominica in 2006.

knowledge that he cried.

"Yeah, I get a little bit sad about it," he said. "It hurt my feelings. When you see a child that needs help and you know if you make a move, you can make it happen . . .

"I went back to the States and started working [on raising money].

"Baseball is not everything in my life. I have a lot of things I worry about, just like I worry about baseball. There's some people out there struggling badly.

"I'm telling you, a bad day at the field is not even close to what they go through. A bad day on the field, you can replace it the following day. Sick people, a sick kid, there is no way to replace that until somebody makes a move to help the children out.

"I think of a bad day at the field

> "IT IS BEAUTIFUL TO GIVE A CHILD BACK HER LIFE. IT'S SOMETHING PRICELESS."
>
> **– JACQUELINE REYES,** WHOSE DAUGHTER, DIANA, WAS BORN WITH A HOLE IN HER HEART

and a good day at a hospital. The good day at the hospital can make your whole year. That's the way things seem like to me."

Nearly 1 percent of children born in the Dominican Republic have some sort of birth defect that requires surgery. Because there is no pediatric cardiac hospital in the country, sometimes a US team of surgeons, in a mission of mercy, will save a few kids in a nation in which more than 1,000 children are in need. Few can afford the $40,000 operation in the United States. In the Dominican, the operation costs $5,000.

But Ortiz came through in the clutch again.

"We've already operated on four children thanks to David Ortiz's sponsorship," said Dr. Pedro Urena, president of Heart Care Dominicana, who studied at Brown University. "Some of the rooms are still under construction."

There are more than 600 children on the Heart Care Dominicana waiting list. "Sometimes they call a family and say, 'Bring your kid in,' and there's this silence and the mother says, 'I wish you called last month, our girl has died,'" said Pelaez. "That's when you have to go on rounds and look at the faces of the kids that you fixed; otherwise, you won't do it anymore."

Reyes was one of the first to benefit from Big Papi's generosity. She was the only one in the still-being-constructed patients' room when Ortiz toured the facility earlier this month. She had a doll, a heart-shaped red pillow, and a smile that lifted everybody's spirits.

Ortiz, who has a natural way with kids, was impressed.

"She was really happy and excited about seeing me," said Ortiz. "She

Ortiz & Friends   0000321

December 7, 2006

PAY   Heart Care Dominicana

$ 200,000.00

ousand and 00/100 Dollars

was thanking me for what I did. When she was thanking me, I was like, 'No, don't thank me, thank New England. Thank the Red Sox and those fans that donated money.'"

The Red Sox Foundation matched funds, and fans, corporate sponsors, and players made up the rest. Ortiz says for him, it's easy.

"The athlete has the capacity to collect money," he said. "I'm really excited about what I'm doing and I'm going to keep on doing it as long as I can."

Recovering in the new cardiovascular unit in the pediatric wing of the hospital known as CEDIMART (Centros de Diagnostico y Medicas y Telemedicina), Reyes acknowledged that she had never seen Big Papi play; she only knew him from commercials and billboards. For this event, the media were out in full force. Ortiz also met the Dominican first lady, Margarita Cedeno de Fernandez, to discuss the plight of Dominican children. She called him a "true ambassador."

Ortiz, looking stylish in a black sports jacket, red shirt, red shoes, designer sunglasses, and turquoise earrings, first visited a packed room with sick kids. It will be the intensive care unit when it is finished. There he signed the oversized $200,000 check.

"Hopefully everything keeps going and the children get better," he said. "Everything is looking good and I see a lot of happy faces out there. God bless you guys."

Then he visited Diana's room.

"I was frightened at first, he's so big," said Diana. "But he was very nice. Afterward I felt so wonderful. He resembles the poor people, the real people. I'll be grateful forever. I'll pray every day that he hits more home runs."

When Big Papi kissed her twice, her eyes lit up brighter than the lights of Estadio Quisqueya, where the local stars play.

She said it was the first time she was kissed by a boy. A very big boy.

Ortiz chatted with her and signed some baseballs for the nurses. Then he was whisked off to the Red Sox Academy near Santo Domingo, where a batting cage was named in his honor.

"What David Ortiz has done for us is something that we never could pay back," said Reyes's mother, Jacqueline, who works on a textile assembly line for $31.58 a week — barely enough to support Diana, buy her medicine, and feed her two baseball-crazed siblings.

"It is beautiful to give a child back her life. It's something priceless. God bless him wherever he is. It's a miracle."

Ortiz says for him, it's a natural thing. His charitable fund-raising seemed to increase after the death of his mother in a car crash in the Dominican Republic in January 2002.

"It comes from my parents, my mom and dad," Ortiz said. "They teach me how to do the right thing. I tried to keep it with myself. Now everybody looks at you like a role model. I don't feel that I am.

"People are needing help and, basically, if you can afford to do something to help somebody out, I don't mind."

In December of 2006, Diana Reyes got to go home, where all the relatives were waiting. She was greeted like Big Papi at home plate after a walkoff home run.

"We celebrated," said Jacqueline Reyes. "I was jumping up and down."

Not surprisingly, Ortiz speaks his mind when he addresses fans during a pre-game ceremony honoring the victims of the Boston Marathon bombings, five days after the attack. "We had never been through what we went through the past week," he said later.

'THIS IS OUR [EXPLETIVE] CITY'

BY JULIAN BENBOW

The emotions had been boiling all week.

A five-day stretch that had been frantic and unsettling had come to an end. So had the search for the suspected perpetrators of the bombings that shook the city not even a week earlier.

Looking out at the faces in the crowd that April day in 2013, people who had come to Fenway Park to escape, to celebrate, and recapture some of the normalcy they had lost, David Ortiz felt what they were feeling.

"This past week, I don't think there was one human being who wasn't affected by what we got going on down here," Ortiz said. "This past week for me, myself, I was very emotional and angry about the whole situation and got to get that out of my chest and make sure our fans and everyone in the nation knows that this is a great nation and part of it was supporting each other when everything went down."

At the end of the ceremony that preceded the Red Sox' 4-3 win over Kansas City, Ortiz's microphone was hot and his words were clear:

"This is our [expletive] city, and nobody is going to dictate our freedom. Stay strong."

He later apologized for the swear, but not the sentiment. But in the wake of incomprehensible terror, the words were forceful, defiant, and proud.

"I'm from the Dominican Republic and the one thing that I always say is me and my family are blessed by being in this country," Ortiz said. "And I love this country and I would do anything for this country. Everybody was one unit and that's what matters."

Preaching the mantra "Boston Strong," the Red Sox took the first steps in helping an embattled city to heal. The team's support added to the solidarity the city had shown all week in the face of tragedy.

Governor Deval Patrick said, "The response of the people in the crowd in the stadium has been the response of people all over the Commonwealth all week and, frankly, all over the world."

Over the course of the pregame

Ortiz's words became a rallying cry, as evidenced six months later when he homered in Game 1 of the World Series; becoming a U.S. citizen in a June 2008 ceremony at the JFK Library.

ceremony, emotions swung from moment to moment.

A montage played on the outfield scoreboards, image after powerful image.

"That video was pretty moving," Sox manager John Farrell said. "When you consider all that has transpired from the celebration of someone finishing a marathon to the devastation that followed that to all the video, if you watched TV the last 36 hours, I think it was all captured in that five-minute video."

Marathon volunteers lined the Green Monster in front of an American flag as wide as the 231-foot long wall.

Ken Shiff and his wife, Beth, were both starting-line volunteers.

They spent the morning of the marathon meeting the elite athletes, talking with runners. Once they were done, they went to the finish line to cheer their friends.

"And then the whole world changed on us," Ken said.

Standing against that wall, they said they felt unified.

"It's so important," said Ken, 59, a Methuen native. "We've been through hell and back to get through this week. And just to come here and be united with all these people who have the same feelings that we have and to know that it's all over and it's all safe again . . ."

Beth, 60, his wife of 37 years, finished his sentence, "It was just amazing."

The Royals and Red Sox stood shoulder to shoulder along the foul lines.

"Guys were fighting back tears on the line," said Sox reliever Andrew Bailey. "I've never been a part of something like that."

For the national anthem, the crowd of 35,152 became a choir, singing all together.

The field was flooded with the faces they had seen endlessly on television over the past four days. Patrick, Boston Police commissioner Edward Davis, and FBI special agent Richard DesLauriers. They joined marathoners Rick Hoyt and his father, Dick, longtime symbols of the sacrifice and resilience, who threw out the

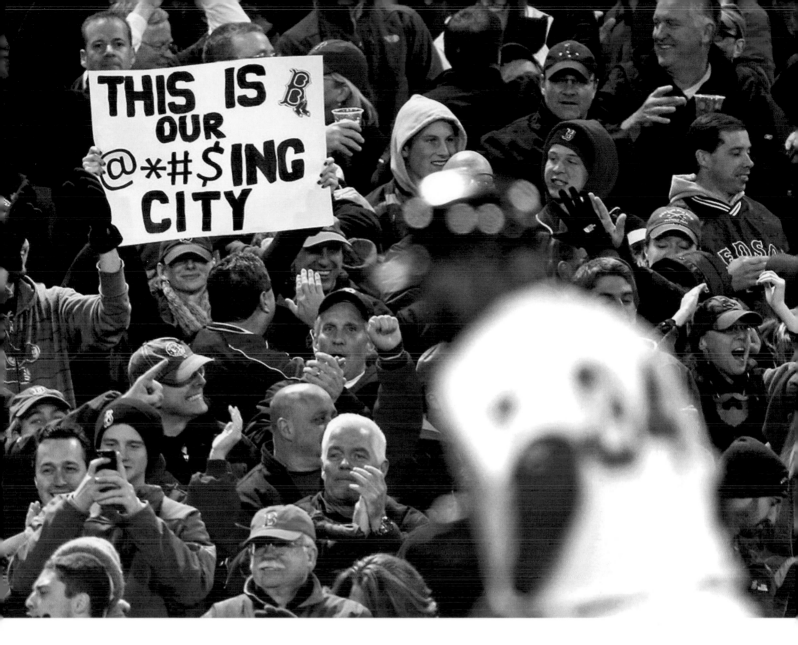

ceremonial first pitch along with off-duty firefighter Matt Patterson and bombing victim Steven Byrne.

Thinking about pitching was almost impossible for starter Clay Buchholz with everything unfolding in front of him.

"I don't think I would've been able to watch it and pitch at the same time," he said. "That was my frame of mind going in. That's the part that I wanted to get through."

One minute everyone in the ballpark was silent, remembering the victims. The next they were applauding the heroes in front of them on the field.

"Then a baseball game breaks out," Jonny Gomes said.

"EVERYBODY WAS ONE UNIT AND THAT'S WHAT MATTERS."

— DAVID ORTIZ

To be able to play, the day after a manhunt left the city all but frozen, was a statement in itself. The scene at Fenway Park on that Friday had been surreal.

"It was just weird to look out the window and not see any action, not see any cars, see any people," third baseman Will Middlebrooks said. "It was like a ghost town. Everyone was on lockdown. It was pretty scary to know I was a couple miles away. I'm just happy it's over."

There were signs of change. Security was heightened. Earlier in the day, police dogs checked the ballpark. Officers in bright yellow jackets seemed to be at every turn. Fans were wan-

ded down at the entrances.

But there were signs that the day obviously meant more.

It took a 4:30 a.m. flight for Neil Diamond to make it to Boston from Los Angeles. Then, he called into the main Fenway Park switchboard and asked if he could sing "Sweet Caroline." The crowd was his choir.

As much as it meant to come away with the win, everyone understood that there was a bigger victory in just being there.

"I wanted to win this game today badly," Ortiz said. "I've had a lot of great moments and emotional situations. Today was different. We had never been through what we went through the past week."

THE LEGACY

BIG PAPI // THE LEGEND AND LEGACY OF DAVID ORTIZ //////////

A two-run homer in July 2016 against the Rays brings a familiar finish. Previous page: Fans walk past a watchful Papi on Yawkey Way.

TO GO WHERE NO DH HAS EVER GONE

BY JOHN POWERS

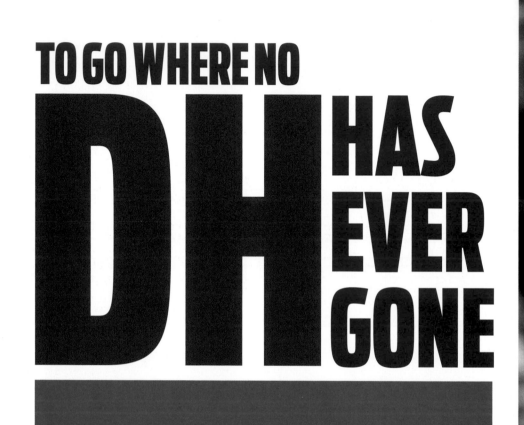

The definitive legacy for all ballplayers is to reach the Hall of Fame, and while his teammates dubbed him "Cooperstown" a while ago, David Ortiz won't find out for at least five years whether he'll join the roster of his sport's bronzed immortals. If elected, Ortiz would become the first designated hitter and only the third native of the Dominican Republic (along with Juan Marichal and former teammate Pedro Martinez) to be enshrined.

While his career numbers clearly measure up (no DH ever has posted better), the essence of Papi's legacy is what he did when the moment beckoned. "I don't do anything but go out there and hit once in a while so I've got to get people to know me," he once observed. "The best way to get people to know me is to produce at the right time."

The right time is October and only three other men, all Yankees, have hit 500 home runs and earned three World Series rings. Babe Ruth, Mickey Mantle and Reggie Jackson played for a dynasty where winning the Fall Classic was considered a birthright. Before Ortiz arrived in the Fens in 2003, Boston hadn't produced a championship since 1918 and had reached the playoffs only six times since 1975. With him at the plate they did it six times in the next seven years and earned two rings.

Much of the difference was due to Ortiz's dramatic knack for extending autumns with one swing. "I've never cried at a baseball game before but I couldn't help it," admitted owner John Henry after Ortiz had driven in the winning runs against Oakland and kept alive the 2003 season – his first with the team.

There was a Ruthian sense of anticipation whenever Papi stepped into the box with a big game on the line and, as often as not, a Ruthian result followed. "I always back it up," Ortiz said. "As long as I've been playing here I've been backing it up."

Since he gave up playing first base on an everyday basis in 2005 and was paid simply to leverage lumber, Ortiz only had a handful of chances per game to deliver, often with men on base. "Hitting is hard, bro," he'd say.

Ortiz did his damage even when rivals lopsided the diamond against him with shifts or wouldn't throw him a strike, preferring to pitch around him, even with slugger Manny Ramirez on deck. "Every year there's something new to

54 HOME RUNS IN 2006, ESTABLISHING A FRANCHISE RECORD

 148 RBIs IN 2005, FOURTH-MOST IN RED SOX HISTORY

figure out," he said. "Every year they find another way to pitch me and I've got to make adjustments…. It never ends, man."

Yet much of Papi's production came after he was 35, when he made the All-Star team four times. "He's still performing at this level all these years later," former Boston general manager Theo Epstein, who signed Ortiz off the street, said after he hit his 500th homer in 2015: "Amazing."

Some skeptics questioned how the same man that the Twins gave up on at 27 could transform himself into one of the game's greatest bashers. While Ortiz's name was leaked in 2009 as one of nearly 100 ma-

jor leaguers who tested positive for performance-enhancing drugs in a 2003 confidential screening, Commissioner Rob Manfred came to Papi's defense in October 2016. Manfred noted that there were at least 10 false positives in the survey testing, adding, "I think it's really unfortunate that anybody's name was ever released publicly." Manfred confirmed that Ortiz has never failed a test since MLB implemented its drug policy in 2004. Ortiz maintains that he is baffled by the positive result from 2003.

The only thing that figures to keep Ortiz out of Cooperstown is if voters conclude that his statistics

were chemically amplified. "If one day I'm up for the Hall of Fame and there are guys who don't vote for me because of that, I will call it unfair," Ortiz said.

The larger practical and philosophical question is whether Ortiz will be able to overcome the traditional balloting bias against DHs, who play in only one league and rarely wear a glove. But in the Hub and elsewhere Papi's legacy has more to do with his sorcery than his statistics. "I would like people to say when they see me walking by: 'There's the guy who made the impossible become possible,'" he said.

> "PEOPLE NEED TO UNDERSTAND THAT WE ARE HUMAN. WE'RE NOT SUPERHEROES. WE HAVE THE SKILLS TO PLAY A SPORT NOT MANY PEOPLE ARE ABLE TO, BUT THAT DOESN'T MEAN WE'RE FROM ANOTHER PLANET. SOMETIMES THINGS COME OUT AND I'LL THINK BACK AND WISH I HAD SAID IT ANOTHER WAY. BUT I DON'T REGRET IT. NEVER."

– DAVID ORTIZ

Clockwise from left: Ortiz checks out the latest hat of a devout fan in 2013; Boston Marathon bombing survivor Patrick Downes, backed by the Achilles Freedom Team, throws out the first pitch to Ortiz in April 2016; adding ring No. 2 in 2007; Hall of Fame numbers and names adorn the ballpark.

LOVE EVERLASTING

BY DAVID FILIPOV

I t might seem wildly off base to suggest that an event in mid-July of 2016 demonstrated David Ortiz's unprecedented status among iconic Boston athletes, given the Red Sox slugger's already teeming résumé of clutch, franchise-altering October performances.

Moreover, it had little to do with Ortiz's statistically historic season for a 40-year-old — an emphatic exclamation point at the end of a Hall-of-Fame-worthy career.

No, it was something that happened before a game on July 19, a day when the nation was reeling from a wave of racially charged violence. Boston police officers, elected leaders, and clergy had assembled on the field at Fenway Park for a moment of silence. But when the announcer called on "our leader, to whom we have turned so many times when the chips were down," it was Ortiz who stepped up to the mike.

His message — "Let's be kind to each other, and choose love" — wasn't as profound as the confirmation it represented of Ortiz's

Clockwise from right: Stalwart Sox fans ceaselessly back Papi; his pregame liner gets lodged in the Pesky Pole in July 2016; throwing out the first pitch with fellow Boston icons Bobby Orr and Bill Russell on Opening Day 2016.

role as a civic leader.

And that, more than anything, indicates why Big Papi has a chance to figure more prominently in Boston after he plays his last game than other local sports legends have.

In this city, the biggest superstars tend to avoid the spotlight when the stadium lights go down. Carl Yastrzemski only reluctantly makes appearances; Larry Bird says he still loves Boston, but we seldom see him when the team he runs, the Indiana Pacers, isn't playing here; Bill Russell and Boston kept each other at arm's length for decades until a recent rapprochement; Bobby Orr, who has handled the glow of retirement as well as anyone, is a distant enough memory that young hockey players have trouble recognizing him.

> "HALL OF FAME PLAYER AND A HALL OF FAME PERSON. THAT'S THE BEST WAY I CAN PUT IT. YOU LOOK AROUND THE GAME AND DAVID IS THE LEADER. HE BRINGS PEOPLE TOGETHER."
>
> — **ADAM JONES,** ORIOLES' OUTFIELDER

But Ortiz goes out of his way to make waves. When, in the wake of the Boston Marathon bombing, Ortiz punctuated his exhortation to a city scarred by terror by shouting an expletive on live TV,

the Federal Communications Commission didn't censure him, it applauded him.

Ortiz is not the only local sports hero to make an important contribution outside the lines — he's not even the greatest Red Sox hitter to do it, not in a world that included Ted Williams, who served in two wars and tirelessly campaigned on behalf of the Jimmy Fund.

Speaking of the Splendid Splinter: Ortiz, while nowhere near as foul-tempered as Williams, has occasionally come off as petty when grumbling about the official scorer or complaining about his contract. Williams was a first-ballot Hall-of-Famer; Big Papi's worthiness as a candidate for baseball's most venerated shrine has been the subject of debate, in no small part because of the allegation of performance-enhancing drug use that he has never cleared up. Another thing regarding Williams: Ortiz refuses to believe that Teddy Ballgame really hit a ball 502 feet, to a spot in the right field bleachers marked by a red seat, a target Papi has been unable to reach, even while taking aim in batting practice.

Where Ortiz tops Ted is the seemingly limitless enthusiasm with which he embraces his role as an all-star ambassador.

It came out July 18, 2016 at a gala for his charity, which raises money to help children in New England and his native Dominican Republic get access to critical pediatric care. Ortiz spoke, without notes, and "had the audience eating out of his hand," according to the Globe's Red Sox beat writer, Peter Abraham.

It came out again two days later, when Ortiz played cheerleader-in-chief during Boston's 11-7 defeat of San Francisco. Big Papi high-fived and hugged the hero of the game, the oft-maligned Hanley Ramirez, jumping up and down on aching, aging feet and legs with an oversized smile, like a father at a Little League game.

It comes out in the little moments before games, when Ortiz chats amicably in Spanish with stadium employees who call out from the seats, or jokes with a woman on crutches about their respective leg ailments.

It helps Ortiz's legacy that his last season is full of moments when he backed up his supersized persona with legendary feats on the field. There was the time in April when he told a sick child he was going to hit a home run for him and then did it.

There was the time he defied the elements in a July 19 game, the night of his "Choose love" speech. In his first at bat, Ortiz hit a ball that died on the warning track, knocked down by a ferocious wind. On his way back to the dugout, Papi pointed an accusing finger into the breeze, as though issuing a challenge to Aeolus himself. His next at bat, with his very next swing, Ortiz drove a 442-foot laser out of the park, a three-run home run that figured prominently in a 4-0 Red Sox win.

Two days later, while launching his usual array of bombs in batting practice, Ortiz hit a ball so hard it got stuck in the metal grill of the right-field foul pole, 302 feet away. The pole bears the name of Johnny Pesky, another beloved Red Sox luminary, whose failure to throw the ball in a critical 1946 World Series moment is

the only dent in his armor; Ortiz is so strong that the ball he unleashed put a dent in Pesky's Pole. Then he hit another home run in the game, a 13-2 Red Sox win.

Ortiz is a superstar, but he's not invincible. When he came up with the bases loaded, no outs, and his team down by a run in the bottom of the ninth the next night, he grounded into a double play and the Sox lost.

Ortiz is ultimately beholden to the rule of "win some, lose some," just like any Boston sports great. Except some of the ones he's won have reversed curses and uplifted an entire city. Which, as much as anything he does with his charity and his dazzling smile after he retires, is why we'll remember him long after the games are over.

Clockwise from below: Hugging daughter Alex, 15, after she sang the national anthem on Opening Day 2016; waving the AL pennant flag in 2013; a family of Papi backers waits to cross Boylston Street; Rod Carew, a Hall-of-Fame hitter, greets Ortiz before a July 2016 game.

FINAL SEASON

BIG PAPI // THE LEGEND AND LEGACY OF DAVID ORTIZ

A NATION SAYS
THANKS

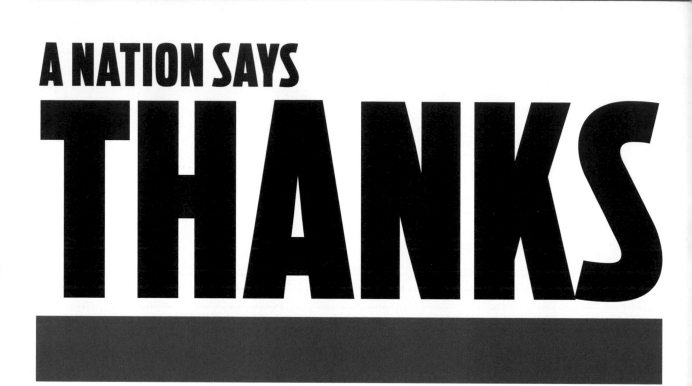

Ortiz celebrates a first-inning homer vs. Colorado in May. Previous page: Ortiz's No. 34 is displayed by bleacher fans holding cards as it is announced that the number will be retired in 2017.

BY JOHN POWERS

David Ortiz knew before the previous season ended that he had only one more left in him. His body felt the accumulated mileage every day. "It's not an easy game to play when you're my age," he said. His rare stint standing sentinel at first base for nine innings stiffened him up like the Tin Man. Even his designated hitter duties required him to arrive at the ballpark by noon for a 7 p.m. game, to limber up. Increasingly, there were more days off to let his sore legs rest and recuperate.

After 19 major-league seasons and a career filled with achievement and honors, Ortiz decided that it would be prudent to retire a bit sooner than later. "I see so many players going out not on their own terms," he mused. "That doesn't look right to me. I think people respect you more if you can do it the way you want."

So on Nov. 18, 2015, his 40th birthday, Ortiz declared that his 20th season and 14th in Boston would be his last. "This is it," he said in a two-minute video. "It was a chapter in my life and I want to go on to the next one. I don't want to be the guy that people feel sorry for."

His valedictory was a hail and farewell that ran from February into October, with his teammates especial-ly motivated to extend it into November. "We're trying to get to the World Series every year," second baseman Dustin Pedroia said during spring training. "But there may be a little added something to get David there one more time. How cool would that be, right?"

Along the way to autumn there were tributes to Ortiz in every city where he was making his final appearance, frequently with charitable donations and almost always with customized keepsakes. A cable-car bell from the Giants. A Stetson cowboy hat from the Astros. Boots emblazoned with BIG PAPI from the Rangers. A surfboard from the Padres. A handmade humidor with 50 Davidoff cigars from the White Sox. There were a Hublot watch and 34 pounds of salmon from the Mariners, his

original club, plus a framed copy of his first professional contract. The Twins supplied a 64-ounce jar of peanut butter, recalling a prank by former teammate Corey Koskie. The Orioles gave him the remains of the dugout phone that he'd shattered with his bat three years earlier, after striking out.

And the Yankees presented him with a leather-bound collection of personal letters from his pinstriped rivals present and past. "Some players are born to be Yankees," Ortiz wrote to them. "I was born to play against the Yankees."

Yet, this was no King for a Day tour. Ortiz still was in the lineup, batting third or cleanup and contributing percussive punctuation to the most remarkable final season in baseball annals. He batted .315, his best number since 2012. His 38 homers and 127 runs batted in were his most in a decade and set major-league records for players 40 and over, as did his doubles (48) and extra-base hits (87).

Papi's final lap was marked by

Ruthian moments, beginning with a homer in his final spring training at-bat. After promising a 6-year-old boy from Cheyenne with a congenital heart defect that he'd hit a home run for him that night, Ortiz hammered a two-run blast to beat the Yankees. "It was God putting his hands on a baseball player," he declared. Then he belted two shots in the Bronx on Mother's Day. "I know she's in a place just watching me," said Ortiz, who ritually looked skyward and pointed both index fingers after crossing the plate, an image that was mowed into the Fenway outfield for the final home series.

In mid-May, after a homer in the third inning and a game-tying triple in the ninth, Ortiz banged a two-out offering for a 420-foot double off the wall to beat the Astros in the 11th. "Just say I'm a bad [deleted]," he proclaimed after the first double-triple-homer outing of his career.

Even batting practice was a must-see event. Before a July date

with the Twins, Ortiz drilled a ball so hard that it was wedged in the Pesky Pole's metal screen. "He puts on a display every day," marveled manager John Farrell. "We're watching history right in front of us, nightly."

Only Ted Williams, who at 42 hit .316 and launched 29 homers, the last in his final at-bat, had gone out with more drama. Williams, though, was playing for a seventh-place club in 1960. Ortiz was a centerpiece of a pennant contender that was bidding to become a remarkable worst-to-first-to-worst-to-first story.

In the second half of September when the Sox won 11 straight against the Yankees, Orioles, and Rays to clinch a playoff spot, Ortiz hit .410 with 13 runs batted in and four homers. The most prodigious of them was a two-run, first-inning, game-winning blast at Tampa Bay that struck the catwalk above the rightfield stands more than 400 feet away. "I felt goose bumps," said first base coach Ruben Amaro Jr.

When the club returned to Fenway for the final weekend of the regular season, Ortiz was feted with a trio of pre-game celebrations that left him both exhilarated and exhausted. "It was unbelievable," he said. "I wasn't expecting so much... Everything went better than perfect. It was very special."

Before the Sunday finale against Toronto, when teammates from the three championship clubs turned up bearing the World Series trophies and Dominican Republic president Danilo Medina threw

IN 2016, DAVID ORTIZ SET SINGLE-SEASON RECORDS FOR PLAYERS AGE

OR OLDER WITH

DOUBLES,

EXTRA-BASE HITS,

HOME RUNS, AND

RBIs

> ## "IMPRESSIVE, MAN. THERE WAS NO BOOING OUT THERE. IT SEEMS LIKE EVERYONE WAS HAPPY THAT I'M LEAVING."
>
> **– DAVID ORTIZ,**
> ON THE OVATION HE RECEIVED IN HIS
> FINAL GAME AT YANKEE STADIUM

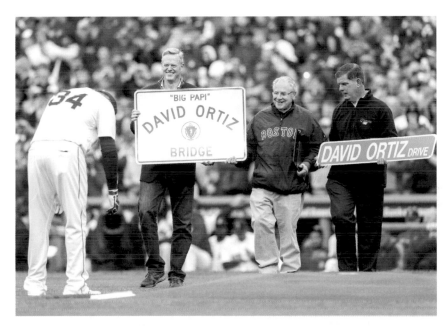

Clockwise from far left: Before his final regular-season game, Ortiz remembers his late mother, Angela; he reacts as Governor Charlie Baker and Boston Mayor Marty Walsh dedicate roadways to him; and teammates past and present fete his exploits, including the 2004 World Series he won with Pedro Martinez.

him the first pitch, Ortiz was presented with a $1 million donation to his Children's Foundation from the Red Sox Foundation and the club's limited partners.

The Sox announced that they would retire his number next season. Governor Charlie Baker said that the state had named the overpass between Kenmore Square and Fenway Park the David Ortiz Bridge, and Mayor Marty Walsh announced that the walkway between the ballpark and the Yawkey commuter rail station would be David Ortiz Drive. "Any time you get bridges and roads named after you, you've obviously got one hell of a legacy," Farrell observed.

The legacy that Ortiz and his teammates most wanted, though, was a fourth ring. "The last day of his career I want to see him holding a trophy and crying," said first baseman Hanley Ramirez. "That is my goal. I want to see him cry. That is the best present we can give him."

NOTE: THIS BOOK WENT TO PRESS AT THE CONCLUSION OF THE 2016 REGULAR SEASON.

Clockwise from right: Ortiz holds USA gymnast Aly Raisman's Olympic medals so she can throw out the first pitch in August; Papi celebrates in New York on Sept. 28 after the Red Sox were assured of first place; Xander Bogaerts cools Ortiz down after Papi went 4-for-4 vs. the Indians in late May; he congratulates Mookie Betts after Betts's first-inning homer against the Twins in July.

Ortiz and Maverick Schutte, 6, of Cheyenne, Wyo., work on their celebration technique as Maverick visits Fenway Park in May.

A HOME RUN FOR MAVERICK

BY RON DRISCOLL

Maverick Schutte's mother makes it very clear that Red Sox Nation has an outpost in Wyoming.

"We're a Red Sox family," said Marti Linnane, whose husband, Mike, is a Portsmouth, N.H., native. "We were married in our Red Sox jerseys. We always watch the games together – it's Maverick's favorite thing to do. We love the Red Sox."

But Maverick is not your average 6-year-old. He is being treated at Denver Children's Hospital and has spent much of his life there. On April 29, 2016, Maverick was having a tough

"YOU TALK ABOUT SUPERHEROES? HE'S A HERO TO BE ABLE TO GET THROUGH ALL THE TOUGH TIMES."

– DAVID ORTIZ

day, so former Red Sox player Kevin Millar, a longtime supporter of the Children's Miracle Network Hospitals, tried to cheer him up.

Before the Red Sox-Yankees game at Fenway Park, Millar filmed a video with David Ortiz to wish Maverick well. Ortiz went even farther, promising that he would hit a home run for Maverick that night.

"When he saw the video he jumped on top of me and hugged me and said, 'This is the best day of my life.' He wouldn't go to bed; he had to watch the game," said Marti. "When David hit the home run, it was such a thrill. We knew why it happened."

Ortiz's "called shot" – the 507th homer of Big Papi's career – was not just any long ball. It came off the Yankees' Dellin Betances, one of the best relievers in the game. Ortiz had been 0 for 7 with four strikeouts against him before the homer, a two-run shot in the eighth inning that won the game, 4-2, for the Red Sox.

When Ortiz hit the home run, he did not remember his promise until he crossed the plate and saw Millar in the stands with his children and pulled them close for a group hug. Later, Ortiz said, "I think God is the one who takes over this stuff."

"Maverick just knew David was going to do it," said Marti. Before

Maverick finally went to bed, he sent a video to Ortiz via Millar.

"Big Papi, you never let me down and you're the best player ever in the Red Sox game and I'm trying the hardest to get out there to Fenway Park and meet you," said Maverick, who has undergone more than 30 surgical procedures and has survived heart failure.

"It was very touching," said Ortiz. "I started thinking about it when I got home. That was when I really was like, 'Wow, I can't believe this really happened.'"

Less than two weeks later, on May 11, Maverick thanked Big Papi in person at Fenway Park, where it didn't take him long to feel at home. Maverick talked with Ortiz and several other players in the clubhouse before being interviewed in the Red Sox dugout, where he playfully took the microphone and conducted his own interviews.

"You're talking about 6 years old and he's been through hell," said Ortiz of Maverick, who wore a Red Sox cap, an Ortiz jersey and Batman Crocs. "You talk about superheroes? He's a hero to be able to get through all the tough times."

"Every day you bump into people complaining about life. When you see things like this, you have to thank God every day for being able to wake up and be healthy."

"YOU EXPECT IT. IN THIS GAME IT'S SO TOUGH TO DO, AND HE MAKES IT LOOK EASY."

— **DUSTIN PEDROIA,** ON ORTIZ'S GAME-WINNING HOMER VS. TORONTO ON SEPT. 30

Clockwise from far left: Mookie Betts and Ortiz go airborne to celebrate Ortiz's final home run, on Sept. 30 at Fenway vs. Toronto; avoiding a foul ball in May; taking a knee and doffing his cap to the fans before his final regular-season game; hanging with Hanley Ramirez at the season opener in Cleveland.

Clockwise from right: A seventh-inning stretch message for Ortiz in his regular-season finale; amid the hoopla, a swing and a miss; a young New Hampshire fan hopes for eye contact; Ortiz steals second after his game-winning double vs. the Astros in May; Fenway fans can't believe their hero is signing off. Previous page: Preparing for a mid-September game vs. Baltimore.

THE NUMBERS

BIG PAPI // THE LEGEND AND LEGACY OF DAVID ORTIZ

DAVID ORTIZ

MR. BIG

NAME: David Americo
(Arias) Ortiz

NICKNAME: Big Papi
(or Cookie Monster)

POSITIONS: Designated
hitter and first baseman

BATS: Left

THROWS: Left

HEIGHT: 6'3"

WEIGHT: 230 lbs.

BORN: November 18, 1975
in Santo Domingo,
Dominican Republic

HIGH SCHOOL:
Estudia Espaillat

DEBUT: September 2, 1997
(Age 21 – 14,750th player
in MLB history)

3 PH

53 1B

HOME RUNS BY POSITION

485 DH

BY RON DRISCOLL

David Ortiz finally gave up chasing Ted Williams. After trying to match it for years, Ortiz voiced his skepticism in 2015 about Williams's 502-foot home run in 1946, even though a lone red seat in a sea of Fenway Park green allegedly pinpoints where the blast landed. Knowing that the Splendid Splinter was revered in these parts as "the greatest hitter who ever lived," Big Papi found a way to forge his own Boston legacy: by winning.

Ortiz racked up glittering offensive numbers, to be sure, some of which eclipsed Teddy Ballgame, Carl Yastrzemski, Jim Rice, and others in the Red Sox pantheon. But the numbers that ultimately mattered most to Big Papi were the three world championships he delivered to a title-starved region that had not celebrated since long before Williams's time. Here are some facts and figures that help bring Ortiz's Fenway tenure into focus.

CAREER MILESTONE HOME RUNS

100

May 28, 2004:
A grand slam off
Seattle's Joel Piniero at
Fenway Park that gave
the Red Sox a 6-4 lead on
the way to an 8-4 victory.

200

June 29, 2006:
A solo homer off the
Mets' Duaner Sanchez in
the eighth inning of a 4-2
Red Sox victory
at Fenway Park.

300

July 9, 2009:
A two-run shot off Kansas
City's Luke Hochevar in
the first inning of an 8-6
loss to the Royals at
Fenway Park.

400

July 4, 2012:
At Oakland's O.co
Coliseum, a solo homer
in the fourth inning
off A.J. Griffin of the
Athletics, who went on to
defeat the Red Sox, 3-2.

500

Sept. 12, 2015:
At Tropicana Field,
the second of two homers Ortiz hit
that day off the Rays' Matt Moore,
a solo shot in the fifth inning of an
eventual 10-4 Red Sox victory.

HOME RUNS
BY TEAM

RED SOX
483

TWINS
58

541
**TOTAL CAREER
HOME RUNS**

BLASTS, YEAR BY YEAR

Year	HR
97	1
98	9
99	0
00	10
01	18
02	20
03	31
★ 04	41
★ 05	47
★ 06	54
★ 07	35
★ 08	23
09	28
★ 10	32
★ 11	29
★ 12	23
★ 13	30
14	35
15	37
★ 16	38

ORTIZ SMASHED AT LEAST **30** HOME RUNS **10** TIMES,

⬆

LEADING THE AMERICAN LEAGUE WITH A CAREER-BEST **54** HOMERS IN 2006.

★ ALL-STAR SEASON   WORLD SERIES WIN

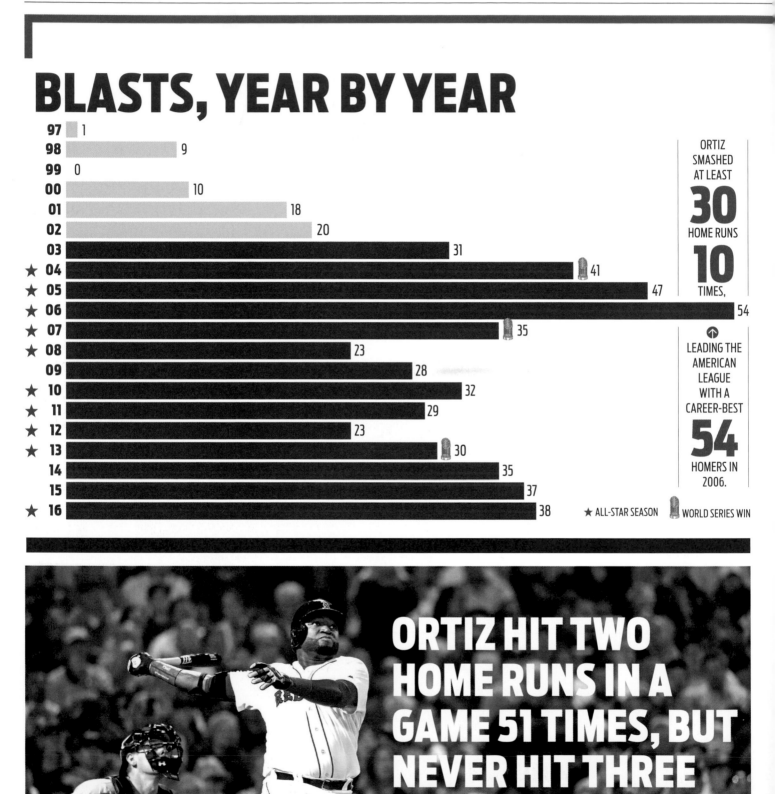

ORTIZ HIT TWO HOME RUNS IN A GAME 51 TIMES, BUT NEVER HIT THREE

FREQUENT VICTIMS

6 HOME RUNS

ROY HALLADAY

5 HOME RUNS

JAMIE MOYER

4 HOME RUNS

12 PITCHERS:
Chris Archer, Ramon Ortiz,
Ervin Santana, Joe Blanton,
A.J. Burnett, Josh Towers,
Mark Buehrle, Matt Garza,
Seth McClung, Kevin Millwood,
Gavin Floyd, Gil Meche

HOME RUNS BY COUNT	
1-1	76
0-0	74
3-2	69
2-2	60
2-1	54
1-0	52
0-1	45
1-2	37
3-1	30
2-0	29
0-2	9
3-0	6

HOME RUNS BY INNING	
1	85
2	37
3	58
4	82
5	73
6	66
7	48
8	48
9	32
Extra	12

HOME RUNS VS. TEAMS	
TOR	62
BAL	55
TBR	53
NYY	53
DET	36
TEX	33
LAA	32
SEA	30
CHW	28
CLE	27

Ortiz hit four career homers vs. Boston, including one off Pedro Martinez and one off Pedro's brother, Ramon.

HOME RUN DESTINATIONS

LF — 39
L-CF — 32
CF — 80
R-CF — 93
RF — 297

120 VS. LHP
421 VS. RHP

CAREER MILESTONES

632
DOUBLES (10TH)

541
HOME RUNS (17TH)

1,768
RBIs (22ND)

4,765
TOTAL BASES (31ST)

2,472
HITS (T-103)

Ortiz homered in 29 ballparks off 27 opponents. He had 11 walk-off homers and 11 grand slams.

30 & 100

David Ortiz is the only player in MLB with 30+ HR and 100+ RBI in each of the last four seasons (2013-2016)... **ORTIZ REACHED THOSE TOTALS 10 TIMES** with the Red Sox, most in club history (Ted Williams ranks 2nd with 7). His 10 Boston seasons of 100 RBI also eclipse Williams (9) for most in franchise history.

THE ONLY PLAYERS WITH AT LEAST 10 SEASONS OF 30+ HR AND 100+ RBI FOR A SINGLE TEAM:

Babe Ruth	12, Yankees
Albert Pujols	10, Cardinals
Hank Aaron	10, Braves
Lou Gehrig	10, Yankees
DAVID ORTIZ	**10, RED SOX**

ALL-TIME HOME RUNS (MLB)

15.	Manny Ramirez	555
16.	Mike Schmidt	548
17.	**DAVID ORTIZ**	**541**
18.	Mickey Mantle	536
19.	Jimmie Foxx	534

ALL-TIME HITS (MLB)

101.	Mickey Vernon	2,495
102.	Fred McGriff	2,490
103.	**DAVID ORTIZ**	**2,472**
	Ted Simmons	2,472
105.	Joe Medwick	2,471

GAMES AT FENWAY

DAVID ORTIZ APPEARED IN 1,014 REGULAR-SEASON GAMES AT FENWAY PARK (BOS-999, MIN-15)... THE ONLY PLAYERS TO APPEAR IN 1,000 REGULAR-SEASON GAMES AT THE VENUE ARE:

CARL YASTRZEMSKI	DWIGHT EVANS	TED WILLIAMS	JIM RICE	DAVID ORTIZ
1,676	1,249	1,165	1,048	1,014

ALL-TIME DOUBLES (MLB)

8.	Carl Yastrzemski	646
9.	Honus Wagner	643
10.	**DAVID ORTIZ**	**625**
11.	Hank Aaron	624
12.	Paul Molitor	605
	Paul Waner	605

ALL-TIME DOUBLES (Red Sox)

1.	Carl Yastrzemski	646
2.	Ted Williams	525
3.	**DAVID ORTIZ**	**524**
4.	Dwight Evans	474
5.	Wade Boggs	422

PAPI'S BIG PAYDAYS *ANNUAL SALARY ONLY

98	$170,000
00	$220,000
01	$260,000
02	$950,000
03	$1,250,000
04	$4,587,500
05	$5,250,000
06	$6,500,000
07	$13,250,000
08	$13,000,000
09	$13,000,000
10	$13,000,000
11	$12,500,000
12	$14,575,000
13	$14,000,000
14	$15,000,000
15	$16,000,000
16	$16,000,000

CAREER — **$159,512,500**

■ MINNESOTA TWINS ■ BOSTON RED SOX

MOST GAMES PLAYED (Red Sox)

1.	Carl Yastrzemski	3,308
2.	Dwight Evans	2,505
3.	Ted Williams	2,292
4.	Jim Rice	2,089
5.	**DAVID ORTIZ**	**1,953**

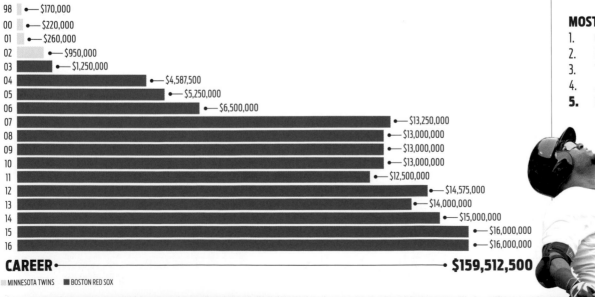

SHARED APPRECIATION

OF THE 27 MEMBERS OF THE 500-HOMER CLUB, FIVE HAVE PLAYED FOR THE RED SOX. DAVID ORTIZ HIT NEARLY 90 PERCENT OF HIS CAREER HOMERS WITH BOSTON.

100%	89.3%	49.4%	41.6%	6.9%
TED WILLIAMS	**DAVID ORTIZ**	**MANNY RAMIREZ**	**JIMMIE FOXX**	**BABE RUTH**
521 HRs with Red Sox	483 HRs with Red Sox	274 HRs with Red Sox	222 HRs with Red Sox	49 HRs with Red Sox

IN 2016, ORTIZ BECAME THE FIRST SOX HITTER WITH

70

OR MORE EXTRA-BASE HITS IN NINE SEASONS, BREAKING A TIE WITH TED WILLIAMS (8 SEASONS).

IN 2016, ORTIZ HELPED THE RED SOX CAPTURE THEIR EIGHTH POSTSEASON BERTH IN 14 SEASONS SINCE HE JOINED THE CLUB IN 2003. IT WAS BOSTON'S 22ND POSTSEASON APPEARANCE ALL-TIME.

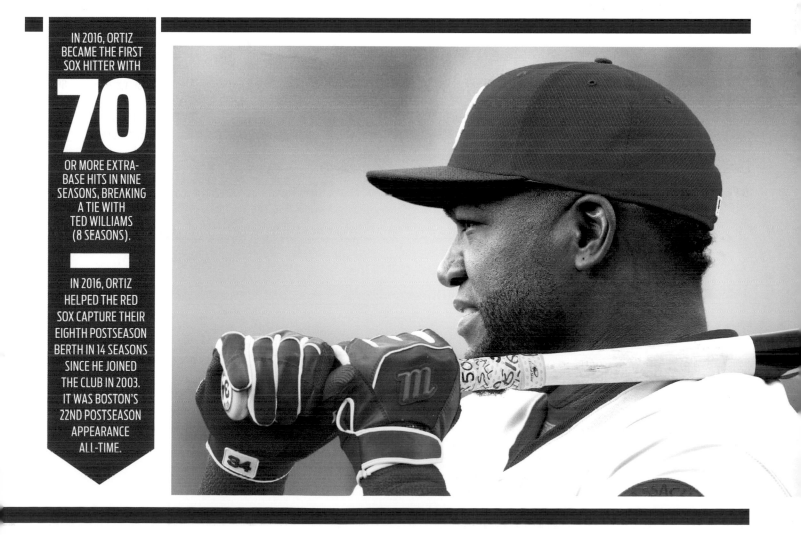

REGULAR-SEASON CAREER

				G	AB	R	H	2B	3B	HR	RBI	SB	CS	BB	SO	BA	OBP	SLG	SH	SF	IBB	Pos	Awards
1997	21	MIN	AL	15	49	10	16	3	0	1	6	0	0	2	19	.327	.353	.449	0	0	0	3/D	
1998	22	MIN	AL	86	278	47	77	20	0	9	46	1	0	39	72	.277	.371	.446	0	4	3	3D	
1999	23	MIN	AL	10	20	1	0	0	0	0	0	0	0	5	12	.000	.200	.000	0	0	0	/D3	
2000	24	MIN	AL	130	415	59	117	36	1	10	63	1	0	57	81	.282	.364	.446	0	6	2	D3	
2001	25	MIN	AL	89	303	46	71	17	1	18	48	1	0	40	68	.234	.324	.475	1	2	8	D/3	
2002	26	MIN	AL	125	412	52	112	32	1	20	75	1	2	43	87	.272	.339	.500	0	8	0	D3	
2003	27	BOS	AL	128	448	79	129	39	2	31	101	0	0	58	83	.288	.369	.592	0	2	8	D3	MVP-5
2004	28	BOS	AL	150	582	94	175	47	3	41	139	0	0	75	133	.301	.380	.603	0	8	8	★D3	AS,MVP-4,SS
2005	29	BOS	AL	159	601	119	180	40	1	47	148	1	0	102	124	.300	.397	.604	0	9	9	★D3	AS,MVP-2,SS
2006	30	BOS	AL	151	558	115	160	29	2	54	137	1	0	119	117	.287	.413	.636	0	5	23	★D3	AS,MVP-3,SS
2007	31	BOS	AL	149	549	116	182	52	1	35	117	3	1	111	103	.332	.445	.621	0	3	12	★D/3	AS,MVP-4,SS
2008	32	BOS	AL	109	416	74	110	30	1	23	89	1	0	70	74	.264	.369	.507	1	3	12	★D	AS
2009	33	BOS	AL	150	541	77	129	35	1	28	99	0	2	74	134	.238	.332	.462	0	7	5	★D/3	
2010	34	BOS	AL	145	518	86	140	36	1	32	102	0	1	82	145	.270	.370	.529	0	4	14	★D/3	AS
2011	35	BOS	AL	146	525	84	162	40	1	29	96	1	1	78	83	.309	.398	.554	0	1	12	★D/3	AS,SS
2012	36	BOS	AL	90	324	65	103	26	0	23	60	0	1	56	51	.318	.415	.611	0	3	13	D/3	AS
2013	37	BOS	AL	137	518	84	160	38	2	30	103	4	0	76	88	.309	.395	.564	0	5	27	★D/3	AS,MVP-10,SS
2014	38	BOS	AL	142	518	59	136	27	0	35	104	0	0	75	95	.263	.355	.517	0	6	22	★D/3	
2015	39	BOS	AL	146	528	73	144	37	0	37	108	0	1	77	95	.273	.360	.553	0	9	16	★D/3	MVP-28
2016	40	BOS	AL	151	537	79	169	48	1	38	127	2	0	80	86	.315	401	.620	0	7	15	★D/3	AS
20 Years				2408	8640	1419	2472	632	19	541	1768	17	9	1319	1750	.286	.380	.552	2	92	209		
162 Game Average				162	581	96	167	43	1	36	119	1	1	89	118	.286	.380	.552	0	6	14		
BOS (14 yrs)				1953	7163	1204	2079	524	16	483	1530	13	7	1133	1411	.290	.386	.570	1	72	196		
MIN (6 yrs)				455	1477	215	393	108	3	58	238	4	2	186	339	.266	.348	.461	1	20	13		

★ INDICATES HE MADE THE AMERICAN LEAGUE ALL-STAR TEAM THAT SEASON, SS=SILVER SLUGGER; MVP-# INDICATES FINISH IN MVP BALLOTING

POSTSEASON CAREER *DOES NOT INCLUDE 2016

	G	AB	R	H	2B	3B	HR	RBI	SB	CS	BB	SO	BA	OBP	SLG	OPS
8 Yrs (17 Series)	82	295	51	87	21	2	17	60	0	1	57	71	.295	.409	.553	.962
8 ALDS	29	106	16	30	9	0	6	16	0	0	21	28	.283	.402	.538	.939
6 ALCS	39	145	21	37	6	2	8	30	0	1	22	38	.255	.357	.490	.846
3 World Series	14	44	14	20	6	0	3	14	0	0	14	5	.455	.576	.795	1.372

CREDITS AND
ACKNOWLEDGMENTS

**BOSTON GLOBE
PHOTOGRAPHS AND
ILLUSTRATIONS BY**

Keith Bedford, 107, 116;
John Bohn, 39; Yoon S. Byun,
41; Barry Chin, 28, 31, 34-35,
38-39, 46, 50-51, 90, 108,
112-113, 116, back cover. Tonia
Cowan, 100; Jim Davis, 4, 6, 7,
13, 23-27, 29-33, 36, 40-41, 43,
46-47, 50-53, 56, 58-59, 61,
66, 72, 77, 85, 90-94, 102, 106,
107-108, 110, 113-114, 116, 122,
124, 127-128; Bill Greene, 40,
42, 47, 50; Pat Greenhouse,
18, 84; Stan Grossfeld, 2, 10,
14, 22, 41-48, 54, 62, 79-81,
98, 127; Matthew J. Lee, 21,
25, 26, 34, 89; Jessica Rinaldi,
83, 96, 121; David L. Ryan, 118;
John Tlumacki, front cover,
31, 40, 44-45, 49, 75, 86, 90,
92, 97, 99, 105, 108, 113, 116,
123, 125; Jonathan Wiggs, 67.

**ADDITIONAL
PHOTOGRAPHS
COURTESY OF**

AP/Wide World Photos, 99
(Elise Amendola); Boston
Red Sox, 8 (Julie Cordeiro), 9
(Brita Meng Outzen); Getty
Images, 1 (Ronald Martinez),
43 (Stephen Dunn), 44 (Al
Bello), 66 (Ezra Shaw), 76
(Jared Wickerham), 109
(Jim McIsaac); Reuters, 69
(Eduardo Munoz).

**WITH SPECIAL
THANKS TO**

Boston Globe publisher John
W. Henry, chief executive
officer Mike Sheehan, and
editor Brian McGrory; Joe
Sullivan and the Globe sports
department; Gordon Edes;
Bill Greene and the Globe
photo department; Lisa
Tuite and the Globe library
staff; Mitch Rogatz, Kristine
Anstrats, and everyone at
Triumph Books; Zachary
Shuster Harmsworth
Literary Agency.